Up and Running

Praise for *Up and Running: Starting and Growing a Leadership Program at a Community College*

"My experience in the Leadership Institute at Community College of Philadelphia was truly remarkable. The opportunity to explore the structure of the College from the position of a student allowed me to gain a fundamental understanding of my own leadership approach as well as the confidence to construct, propose, support, and implement new ideas and initiatives. When I eventually took the role of Department Chair, the leadership training and skills that I developed in that program were immediately and immensely beneficial."—**Sarah Iepson, PhD, associate professor of art history, Art and Design Department Chair, Community College of Philadelphia**

"Drs. Tobia and Gay present a tactical and nimble "how-to" approach to developing a successful leadership development program on college campuses. Much of what the authors highlight is well supported by various data sources, but what is most compelling is that the discourse often focuses heavily on leadership pipeline development in the abstract or in support of national programs that may be fiscally out of reach for many community colleges and smaller private institutions. Using their institution's model, Tobia and Gay offer a practical and successful alternative which can easily and feasibly be replicated at other community colleges or adapted to a variety of other higher educational contexts."—**Nicole Stokes-DuPass, PhD, associate vice president, Institutional Effectiveness & Diversity; professor of sociology, Holy Family University; Pennsylvania State Chairperson, American Council on Education Women's Network (PA ACE)**

Up and Running

Starting and Growing a Leadership Program at a Community College

Susan J. Tobia
Judith L. Gay

AMERICAN ASSOCIATION OF COMMUNITY COLLEGES

ROWMAN & LITTLEFIELD
Lanham • Boulder • New York • London

Published by Rowman & Littlefield
An imprint of The Rowman & Littlefield Publishing Group, Inc.
4501 Forbes Boulevard, Suite 200, Lanham, Maryland 20706
www.rowman.com

Unit A, Whitacre Mews, 26-34 Stannary Street, London SE11 4AB

Copyright © 2018 by Susan J. Tobia and Judith L. Gay

All rights reserved. No part of this book may be reproduced in any form or by any electronic or mechanical means, including information storage and retrieval systems, without written permission from the publisher, except by a reviewer who may quote passages in a review.

British Library Cataloguing in Publication Information Available

Library of Congress Cataloging-in-Publication Data

Names: Tobia, Susan J., 1946- author. | Gay, Judith L. (Judith Lisa), 1950- author.
Title: Up and running : starting and growing a leadership program at a community college / Susan J. Tobia, Judith L. Gay.
Description: Lanham : Rowman & Littlefield, [2018] | Includes bibliographical references and index.
Identifiers: LCCN 2018001341 (print) | LCCN 2018011040 (ebook) | ISBN 9781475839586 (electronic) | ISBN 9781475839562 (cloth : alk. paper) | ISBN 9781475839579 (pbk. : alk. paper)
Subjects: LCSH: Community college administrators—In-service training. | Community colleges—Employees—In-service training. | Educational leadership—Study and teaching. | Teams in the workplace.
Classification: LCC LB2341 (ebook) | LCC LB2341 .T598 2018 (print) | DDC 378.1/01—dc23
LC record available at https://lccn.loc.gov/2018001341

∞ ™ The paper used in this publication meets the minimum requirements of American National Standard for Information Sciences Permanence of Paper for Printed Library Materials, ANSI/NISO Z39.48-1992.

Printed in the United States of America

Dedicated to our moms who believed in and inspired us

Contents

Foreword	ix
Preface	xi
Acknowledgments	xiii
Introduction	xv

Part I: Nuts and Bolts — 1
1 Recruitment and Application — 3
2 Program Schedule, Presenters, and Readings — 7
3 Budget — 15
4 Thinking Styles and Team Building — 21
5 Team Projects — 33

Part II: Key Leadership Content Areas — 43
6 Conflict Resolution — 45
7 Decision Making — 53
8 Diversity and Inclusion — 61

Part III: Evaluation and Sustainability — 69
9 Is It Working? — 71
10 Beyond the Leadership Program — 77

Concluding Thoughts and Overall Summary — 81
Appendix A: Sample Acceptance Letter — 83

Appendix B: Sample Rejection Letter	85
Appendix C: Sample Application	87
Appendix D: Guidelines for the Selection Committee and Selection Criteria	91
Appendix E: Selection Criteria Grid	95
Appendix F: Sample Program Schedule	97
Appendix G: Community College of Philadelphia Leadership Institute Presenters	103
Appendix H: Sample Reading List	107
Appendix I: Checklist for Planning a Leadership Program	111
Appendix J: Descriptors for de Bono's Six Thinking Hats	113
Appendix K: Four Keys to a Successful Six Thinking Hats (STH) Session	115
Appendix L: Sample Project Directive	117
Appendix M: Project Overview Guide	121
Appendix N: Sample Invitation to Project Presentations	123
Appendix O: Sample Project Presentation Feedback Form	125
Appendix P: Final Report Specs	127
Appendix Q: Sample of Projects Completed at Community College of Philadelphia	129
Appendix R: Sample Mentor Request Letter	133
Appendix S: Sample Pre/Post Self-Assessment Tool	135
Appendix T: Session Feedback—Decision Making in Higher Education	137
Appendix U: Rating Summary of Session Topics	139
Appendix V: Sample Midpoint Evaluation	141
Appendix W: Sample Final Evaluation	145
Appendix X: Proposal for Executive Leadership Institute	147
References	151
Index	155
About the Authors	159

Foreword

The 2012 American Association of Community Colleges (AACC) 21st Century Commission on the Future of Community Colleges report recommendations made it clear that the nation's community colleges needed to step up efforts aimed at student success and completion. A subsequent AACC survey of community college CEOs revealed that about 75 percent of community college CEOs surveyed planned on retiring within 10 years. Together these reports made very clear that community colleges needed very deliberate and focused efforts to ensure a new generation was prepared to lead community colleges.

We knew we had to work hard and work fast to prepare new leaders if our sector was going to survive into the future. AACC's leadership development programs, including the John E. Roueche Future Leaders Institute and the Future Presidents Institute, are aimed at helping people to lead from where they are and preparing them to lead in the position they want to attain.

To supplement national training programs, such as AACC's, many community colleges have implemented their own leadership institutes. These "grow-your-own" programs are a critical investment in the success of an institution—an investment that pays off in the present and far into the future. Developing leaders across the entire institution—from customer service staff, to faculty, to senior-level administrators—can lead to increased engagement, more innovation, and, when the time comes, smoother staff transitions. It cannot be overstated how important it is for CEOs to fill their bench with skilled and talented employees. Leadership development is a core principle for AACC and we continue to shine a spotlight on these "grow-your-own" programs in our virtual 21st Century Center.

The "why" of starting a leadership program is easy; the "how" is more difficult. *Up and Running: Starting and Growing a Leadership Program at a*

Community College is an excellent primer. The authors, Drs. Susan Tobia and Judith Gay, were both instrumental in the development and launch of Community College of Philadelphia's successful Leadership Institute in 2002.

In this book, they offer the nuts and bolts of beginning a leadership program, and discuss the lessons they learned with CCP's Institute, including developing selection criteria for participants, budgeting for the program, and creating a curriculum that's beneficial to everyone involved. Drs. Tobia and Gay also understand that learning cannot stop when the Institute ends. They offer advice for helping leaders continue to grow and learn so they can remain engaged and excited.

We have much in common when it comes to forwarding the leadership development initiative. Be it national or local, the focus on community college leadership is critical to the success of our students, our community colleges, and our country.

—Walter G. Bumphus, PhD
President and CEO, American Association of Community Colleges

Preface

A belief in the importance of professional development for all employees, coupled with the anticipated retirement in the coming decade of leaders at community colleges, drove the creation of the Leadership Institute at Community College of Philadelphia in 2002. The goal was to develop and sustain leaders to meet new challenges in an era of rapid change. The institution's leadership understood it must think forward and develop leaders with skills that would strengthen their ability to carry out the college mission and values regarding access and success.

The need for leadership development programs in community colleges is a continuing one. As Ebbers, Conover, and Samuels (2010) note, there is an acceleration in retirement across all leadership levels of community colleges. Terry O'Banion of National American University noted that 75% of presidents have announced plans to retire in the next 10 years, as have 75% of senior administrators.

> Community colleges have finally been recognized by [U.S.] presidents, by legislators, by foundations, by policy centers, by business and industry as one of the most important democratic institutions in the world that is helping to improve our economy and meet the needs of citizens. And at a time we're finally recognized, we've failed to keep up with the preparation of leaders to take on the leadership role. (O'Banion, as cited in Smith, 2016)

The American Association of Community Colleges (AACC) maintains a database that tracks transitions in leadership positions. From 2011 to 2015, the number of transitions increased from 134 to 269.

In 2016, AACC formed the Commission on Leadership and Professional Development to review leadership competencies and leadership needs. They are working to map out options for training opportunities in various areas of higher education, including academic affairs, student affairs, administrative affairs, and advancement. The goal is to help aspiring leaders understand the pathways available to leadership positions (Ullman, 2017).

Community College of Philadelphia's Leadership Institute addresses the ongoing leadership gap. A finalist for the 2005 Bellwether Award, the Leadership Institute was featured in *Growing Your Own Leaders: Community Colleges Step Up* by Carol Jeandron (2006). The Institute encourages faculty, staff, and administrators from various areas of the college to develop and enhance their leadership skills through an academic year program that includes workshops, readings, and networking with leaders external and internal to the institution. Participants also work collaboratively on a team project tied to the college mission and strategic goals.

This book will serve as a resource for community college leaders and others who would like to start their own leadership programs and current program coordinators interested in expanding their program ideas. It addresses goals, process, structure, timeline, resources, key leadership topics, impact, and lessons learned.

Acknowledgments

The opportunity for professional development to enhance leadership skills and to grow new leaders was a signature piece of Stephen M. Curtis's platform when he served as president of Community College of Philadelphia. So when he charged then vice president for Academic Affairs Judith Gay to start a leadership program, we were very excited. A small group began to research leadership programs at other community colleges and finding only a few, we began to develop our own. It was at this time that Susan Tobia had the opportunity to spend a year as an American Council on Education Fellow. That year was a pivoting one for her as she gained incredible knowledge about leadership in higher education and brought back to the institution much of what she had learned. Susan is especially grateful to Marlene Ross, then Director of the Fellows program, for her inspiration and wise guidance which continues to have an impact to this day.

We also want to acknowledge Donald Generals, the current president of Community College of Philadelphia, for his enthusiasm and continuing support of the Leadership Institute. The coordinators of the Leadership Institute for the past 13 years have come from the faculty, academic affairs, student affairs, institutional advancement, and multimedia services. We want to express appreciation to Joan Johnson, Mary Griffin, Brian Seymour, Peter Baratta, Matthew Shupp, Tarsha Scovens, Lynne Sutherland, Kristin Starr, and Allan Kobernick. Their expertise, energy, and commitment are beyond comparison, and we are indebted to them for their leadership.

The Institute engaged external presenters who enriched program participants with their experience and wisdom. We want to especially thank Deb Cummins Stellato, Thomas A. Gordon, and Ana Maria García for their incredible contributions and insights shared with the many Institute cohorts over the years. They brought strength and courage to us all. We are also thankful for the generosity of our presenters from within the college who shared their expertise in finance, grant writing, public speaking, decision making, and assessment. And we are appreciative for those colleagues who gave of their time and energy to serve as mentors to Institute participants as they worked through their projects.

A debt of gratitude is extended to Pete Watkins, a former colleague, who graciously agreed to read the book draft and provide his eagle-eye feedback. We are also grateful to Rowman & Littlefield for agreeing to publish our book and to Sarah Jubar and Emily Tuttle, our editors, who exhibited the utmost clarity in their expectations and who graciously gave of their time and advice throughout the writing process.

We want to thank all the Leadership Institute alumni who shared their precious time with us, who contributed their ideas, who trusted us with their honesty, and who showed us that leadership programs do make a difference. Their growth, both personally and professionally, has enriched our institution, other institutions, and their communities. In the end, it is these leaders who will serve to meet the challenges of higher education now and in the future.

Introduction

This book is primarily a "how-to" guide for setting up and sustaining a leadership program in alignment with an institution's mission and goals reflected in such documents as its strategic plan or academic master plan. Thus, Part I of the book begins with a step-by-step process in suggested sequence from the recruitment/application process to team building and the team projects.

Since content is also an essential element, Part II highlights some key conceptual areas to be considered in developing leadership, including conflict resolution, decision making, and diversity/inclusion in higher education. These areas were chosen because they were consistently addressed in Community College of Philadelphia's Leadership Institute in ways that had a positive impact on participants.

Part III addresses evaluation and sustainability both for the program and for the program alumni. Changes made and insights gained along the way are offered to readers throughout the book.

PART I: NUTS AND BOLTS

In any institution, issues arise that call for leadership in various contexts, whether it be taking on a new orientation program for new students, initiating an enrollment assistance center, leading groups of faculty members in teaching circles, or developing a customer-service plan. Thus it is important to develop leaders across the institution and at all levels (faculty, staff, administrators) and provide them an opportunity to network with colleagues with different thinking styles and across divisions. It is also important to broaden people's perspectives by exposing them to local, state, and national issues affecting higher education. A well-sequenced plan with a defined structure and process is critical to providing an effective leadership program.

PART II: KEY LEADERSHIP CONTENT AREAS

Leadership programs provide opportunities for participants to learn about, practice, and reflect on skills related to important content areas such as conflict resolution, decision making, and diversity/inclusion. These topics are often at the top of lists for incorporation in leadership development programs. Programs can also encourage participants to consider the impact of their actions on others within their departments and across the institution. As Warren Bennis (2009) suggests, to be a successful institution, there is not only a need for leaders to do things right but also to do the right thing.

PART III: EVALUATION AND SUSTAINABILITY

As with any successful program, it is important to take periodic pulses along the way. This may be accomplished through various methods, including written and oral evaluative feedback, questionnaires, and interviews. For Community College of Philadelphia's Leadership Institute, we ask participants to write evaluative and reflective responses after each monthly session, at the midpoint, and at the conclusion of the program. What we learn motivates both short-term and long-term changes.

Part I

Nuts and Bolts

Chapter One

Recruitment and Application

LEARNING GOALS

- Consider options for matching selection of participants with the purpose and goals of the leadership program.
- Gain ideas for establishing a timely application and selection process.

RECRUITMENT

Many leadership initiatives aim to help the middle- or senior-level administrators move into higher positions. Fewer programs seem to tap into the great interest that people from all levels of the institution have in gaining leadership skills either for personal benefit or for the opportunity to engage in greater leadership responsibilities within their professional areas.

It is important for colleges initiating a leadership program to match participants with its purpose and goals. Potential populations are faculty serving or preparing to serve as department heads, employees in executive leadership positions, or customer-service staff. At Community College of Philadelphia (CCP), we value including people at all levels of the institution. Given the diversity of service in the public community college, it is critical that the various units within the college have knowledge of each other's functions and interact effectively.

Recruiting a mix of faculty, staff (hourly workers), and administrators from multiple areas of the institution ensures a positive impact on each person's understanding of the organizational culture and encourages them to network with other colleagues. Working more effectively across units leads to a more positive experience for both employees and the students served.

Recruitment for a leadership program should be done well in advance to afford ample time for dissemination of information, feedback, and responses to questions. Announcements on the college website or outreach via email may occur up to a year in advance. For first-time programs, it is important to offer information workshops that include the president or senior leadership. Such inclusion speaks to the significance of buy-in from the leadership of the institution for the initial program and its sustainability.

For established programs, a video with highlights from the program may be utilized to inspire interest. The testimony of program alumni via website or in person is another recommended strategy. Alumni experiences are powerful tributes in encouraging others to consider applying. At CCP, applicants often stated that they applied because of the positive experiences of their department colleagues. (See textbox 1.1 for a sample quote.) A third strategy is personal outreach to college employees who have exhibited interest in the past or who demonstrate leadership skills.

"I was invited to attend two Leadership Institute events by two different people. . . . My decision was finalized by the very positive accounts of experiences from various alumni and the recruiting video."—CCP Participant

APPLICATION

Full-time faculty, administrators, and staff (hourly workers) who are interested in seeking leadership positions in the future or honing their leadership skills for the positions they currently hold are invited to apply. Part-time faculty, administrators, and staff who have been continuously employed at the college for a minimum of 2 years may also apply. A 2-year minimum provides some insurance that an applicant has a modicum of investment in the institution.

If the program begins at the start of the academic year (August/September), notice of the application should be published in early spring (March) with a deadline for submission in May. Applicants are then notified in June. (See Appendix A for a sample acceptance letter.) This gives those accepted time to complete preparatory requirements. For example, they may have a reading assignment or they may need to complete a thinking-style inventory. If an applicant is not accepted, a letter should be sent with an explanation and suggestions for strengthening the application should the applicant choose to reapply in the future. Such encouragement keeps the door open for reconsideration. (See Appendix B for a sample rejection letter.)

The application consists of essays, recommendations, a signature of commitment, and résumé. (See Appendix C for a sample application.) Candidates should demonstrate potential for assuming leadership roles within the college community. One way they may show this is by identifying a professional situation where they took a leadership role and reflecting on the effectiveness or ineffectiveness of the leadership strategies employed in the situation. (See textbox 1.2 for a sample quote.) Candidates should also provide evidence of service to the college community and/or the community at large in some leadership capacity.

> "Very early on in my time as department head . . . my first instinct was to think that my job was to do it all myself, but trying to do this led to several problems. First, I simply could not effectively resolve all the items on my desk, particularly because matters were often time sensitive. More significantly, even if I could do all the work in an excellent fashion on my own, I now see that I would surely not be handling myself as a genuine leader. Leaders do not merely get things done; they empower others to work with them to accomplish great things."—CCP Participant

All candidates should receive the approval of their supervisors to participate in the program if selected. Supervisor buy-in is important to a person's consistent participation and completion of the program. A supervisor may even be the catalyst for a person to apply. If that is the case, he or she may be more motivated to support both the employee's participation in the program and his/her greater leadership role in the department upon completion. If the candidate is a faculty member, the department chair may be able to arrange a teaching schedule that allows the faculty member to participate.

For first-time programs, a selection committee should consist of senior leadership or college employees connected with the targeted population of participants. Starting in the second year, committee members, including a senior leader and three former leadership program participants representing various college constituents, separately review and rank the applications using established criteria. (See Appendix D for selection committee guidelines and Appendix E for a sample criteria grid.) A recommended goal is that faculty, staff, and administrators from diverse cultural backgrounds and who serve in various roles within the institution are represented. This is designed to help ensure that

- Multiple perspectives are brought to bear on the issues addressed in the leadership program.

- Participants will be able to share both breadth and depth of knowledge of the college as an institution.
- Participants have opportunities to form working relationships with colleagues outside their own areas.
- Communication and cooperation among employees in different areas of the college will be greatly improved over time as the program is repeated.

LESSONS FROM COMMUNITY COLLEGE OF PHILADELPHIA

Initially, the total number of participants in the Leadership Institute was set at 20. As we developed and added more focused team projects, a discussion board, mentors, and a shadowing experience, we found that a group of 12–15 was a better target. A smaller group provided easier accessibility to authentic discussion, more time with coordinators and team members, and the opportunity to develop stronger community affiliation.

We also learned how critical it was to elicit a strong commitment to the schedule for those selected to the Institute. Participants signed off on their commitment on the application, and they were reminded of this commitment in their acceptance letters. The commitment of participants to be present at each meeting was important, not only to their progress but also to the strength and trust of the Institute community. The first session was particularly significant as it was a full day and was the point at which the group established itself and set goals for how they would work together throughout the year. If a person could not attend the first session, he or she was asked to defer to another year.

SUMMARY OF IDEAS

1. Define your population and a target for the number of participants.
2. Establish a timeline for the recruitment and application process.
3. Ensure the application provides adequate information for selection of candidates.
4. Develop selection criteria that match your purpose and goals.
5. Obtain the firm commitment of participants and supervisors.

Chapter Two

Program Schedule, Presenters, and Readings

LEARNING GOALS

- Consider options for programming, including structure and content.
- Gain ideas from one college's leadership program experience.

The major purpose of a community college leadership program is to develop leaders within the college community by fostering the ability of individuals to meet institutional challenges in an era of rapid change. A priority in starting and sustaining a program is the commitment of senior leadership, starting with the president. This commitment includes not only a philosophical one but a financial one as well.

At Community College of Philadelphia, it was actually a former president who inspired the initiation of the Leadership Institute and provided support for it. His continuing endorsement in words and action created enthusiasm for the program across the institution, and the program became an institutional marker for the importance of leadership development. Community College of Philadelphia's current president has continued to support the program, which is in its 13th year.

The Institute incorporates a variety of speakers, topics, readings, and activities designed to enhance leadership skills by providing participants with opportunities in the following areas:

The Field and Context Within Which We Work

- To develop a deeper understanding of the college mission, vision, and values
- To gain insight into the organizational structure and organizational culture
- To interact with and gain insight from leaders in various fields related to the mission of the community college
- To increase awareness of the local, state, and national contexts within which the college functions
- To increase understanding of specific ways in which the larger environment may impact the college in the pursuit of its mission

The Nature of Leadership

- To increase knowledge of resource allocation, budgeting, and finance
- To study decision making in the context of individual and institutional values
- To develop increased self-awareness as leaders, enhance communication skills, and learn new strategies for conflict resolution

Working With Others

- To become part of a diverse, collaborative network of problem solvers
- To work collaboratively on a project of interest to the participant and of benefit to the college community

PROGRAM SCHEDULE AND PRESENTERS

A program to develop leaders is best delivered through sustained experiences and opportunities over an extended period. At Community College of Philadelphia, in 10 sessions between August and May, a selected cohort of faculty, administrators, and staff meet monthly to learn about the internal and external issues impacting the college and to reflect on their leadership roles within the organization. Approximately 45 hours of presentations and in-depth workshops include topics such as diversity/inclusion, fiscal management, thinking styles, decision making, conflict resolution, and presentation skills.

Participants are further engaged through interactive presentations with local, state, and national leaders. Each session begins with lunch and a discussion of readings followed by a presentation, response to presenters, project updates, and evaluation. (See Appendix F for a sample schedule.)

It is recommended that the opening session focus on building community among participants. This is a full-day session at on off-campus site which provides the cohort an opportunity to get to know one another and to think about how it wants to function as a group. Having the session off campus provides participants a chance to step away from their daily responsibilities and routines and to think in broader terms about their leadership possibilities at the institution. Because this session is so critical in building trust and understanding the level of commitment required for a successful experience, anyone who cannot make this session is asked to defer participation to another year.

Two examples of exercises that assist in building community and commitment are the Name Tent and Metaphor Exercises. In the Name Tent Exercise, participants develop group guidelines to help them function in an optimal way. All groups operate under guidelines, whether explicit or implicit. It is wise to establish operational guidelines from the beginning to ensure that everyone is comfortable within the group and feels free to express, question, and openly chew on ideas that surface about leadership.

One way to do this is to have participants break into smaller groups of four or five (depending on the size of the cohort) and create five or six guidelines. Each smaller group then shares their guidelines with the whole group. These are written on a flip chart, and the guidelines to which everyone agrees become the cohort operational guidelines. They are written on the back of each participant's name tent for continual reference during sessions. (See textbox 2.1 for a sample of group guidelines.)

SAMPLE GROUP GUIDELINES

- Open communication to include clarity and authenticity
- Respect for individuals
- Confidentiality
- Support for each other
- Availability to one another, including openness to ideas

The Metaphor Exercise is a fun way to spark discussion on leadership characteristics. In their applications, participants write about the leaders they most admire and comment on their leadership qualities. A summary of their responses is shared with the group. In the Metaphor Exercise, participants organized in small groups (with different membership from the previous exercise) are given six stems to complete. (See textbox 2.2 for examples of stems.)

Each small group completes the stems and then chooses their two best sentences for each stem that identify characteristics of leadership. These are shared with the larger group along with explanation and discussion. A summary of the responses is provided prior to the next session. Participants can periodically refer to these characteristics as they think about leadership from local and national levels and as they reflect on their own leadership qualities as well as those they aspire to develop.

SAMPLE STEMS FOR METAPHOR EXERCISE

- Leadership is a pie because . . .
- Leadership is the weather because . . .
- Leadership is a balloon because . . .
- Leadership is a celebration because . . .
- Leadership is a mirror because . . .
- Leadership is a shoe because . . .

Some examples of completed stems are

- Leadership is a pie because a leader must be crusty at times.
- Leadership is a balloon because a leader must rise above to get a clear view of the situation.
- Leadership is the weather because a leader has to prepare for change.

Case studies from *The Leadership Dialogues* by Tyree, Milliron, and de los Santos (2004) are also good entry exercises into the consideration of leadership characteristics. Participants are provided with questions to prompt them to think about how they would respond in given situations.

The opening session also includes a discussion of the results of the selected thinking-styles inventory. An external presenter with expertise in thinking styles and teamwork provides an overall explanation of the results, and participants are given time to reflect on and share their results with others. Information from the inventory is later used in forming project teams.

The remaining fall sessions are devoted to delineating issues relevant to the mission of the community college at the local, state, and national levels. This environmental context provides a framework for understanding a specific institution's role in the higher education arena. Information gleaned from these sessions also provides a "big picture" context for participants' work at the department levels as well as their work on the team projects.

Local leaders invited to present include those from the mayor's office, the school district, and major city initiatives. To provide a state perspective, a panel of presidents from area community colleges offers participants frank discussions of difficult issues faced by leaders and the opportunity to share ideas and strategies for addressing them. They also share their stories about their career paths to the college presidency, their leadership/management styles, and what keeps them awake at night. National presenters include heads of organizations such as the American Association of Community Colleges, the Association of Community College Trustees, and the U.S. Department of Education. The support of the college president and other senior leaders is instrumental in enlisting such presenters.

Connections with leaders outside the college not only enhance the college's image but, especially for local leaders, also expose them to college initiatives, providing a firsthand experience of the college mission. This has potential for increased impact when it comes time for funding decisions, which are often enhanced by building relationships. Hearing from community college presidents illuminates the economic and political issues of leadership and illustrates how the demands and needs of the workforce are increasingly major factors in the courses developed. National presenters provide a broader view and enable participants to see how their specific institution fits into the overall fabric of higher education.

The spring sessions are devoted to developing leadership skills. Presenters selected are those with expertise in communication and conflict resolution, decision making, presentation skills, assessment, budget, and diversity/inclusion in higher education. All presenters are vetted and have extensive experience in leadership capacities. (See Appendix G for list of presenters.)

READINGS

A selected book on leadership should be assigned in the summer prior to the program. This book should

- be accessible to participants from a variety of levels at the institution,
- reflect major issues of leadership that the program will address throughout the year,
- be practical, and
- spark discussion to move participants beyond their current understanding of leadership roles in organizations.

This book is discussed early in the program and remains a reference throughout the remaining sessions.

Additional readings are assigned prior to each session to provide background and an opportunity to reflect on the session's topic. (See Appendix H for a sample list of readings.) Participants utilize a discussion board to reflect as a group on the ideas presented. Each participant has the opportunity during the year to lead or co-lead a reading discussion. The discussion leader is asked to develop two or three questions for the group members to respond to on the discussion board and then to facilitate a discussion during lunch at the start of each session to further develop thinking about the readings. Guidelines for questions and discussion include

- Develop a question or questions that provide room for reflective thought. You may preface the question(s) with a brief summary of the author's point or an introductory statement about your own "take" on the reading to set the context for your question(s).
- Try to relate the question(s) to one of the leadership program goals and/or to your college setting (no names or units identified).
- Submit your question(s) to the program coordinators for feedback by the date designated in order to provide adequate time for your colleagues to respond.
- Review your colleagues' postings prior to the discussion.
- Facilitate the lunch discussion (20–30 minutes).

LESSONS FROM COMMUNITY COLLEGE OF PHILADELPHIA

The sequence of sessions should be strategic. At first, we were focused on a series of topics that we thought would be beneficial to developing leaders but did not give as much thought to the interrelationship of topics. We learned that sessions are more effective if they build on and complement each other.

For example, we placed sessions concerning environmental scanning (local, state, and national) up front so that participants have a broader perspective when examining issues more specific to our college. Participants learn about grant writing in the early stages of their project proposals so they can incorporate some of the funding language and proposal structure. We added a public-speaking session prior to the college-wide presentations of project proposals. Anxiety expressed about public speaking is common, so providing some guidance and techniques was useful, and participants had the opportunity to apply what they learned immediately.

We added an option to give participants the opportunity to shadow senior leadership for a day or longer depending on the situation. This experience provides a full-throttle view of real-time situations in leadership and gives participants a personal feel for the rewards and challenges of leadership. One Institute faculty member shadowed the vice president for Government Relations, which enabled him to learn about an area of the college that was not on his radar but that he came to appreciate in its role as connecting the needs of the city with the educational goals of his own students. He also had the opportunity to meet Arne Duncan, the U.S. Secretary of Education at the time, and to gain additional insights at a national level.

Another Leadership Institute member who worked in the controller's office shadowed the vice president for Planning and Finance which led to her participation in a series of yearlong meetings at the VP level and eventually to her promotion as well as to her completion of her bachelor's degree in accounting.

OPERATIONAL

In the spirit of offering a nuts-and-bolts guide to developing a program, a "Checklist for Planning a Leadership Program" is provided in Appendix I. Generally, it is recommended that program coordinators work as much as a year in advance to secure presenters, especially those external to the institution (may require more advance planning for the national presenter), select reading materials, reserve rooms, and reach a budget agreement.

SUMMARY OF IDEAS

1. Obtain a firm commitment to the leadership program from the president of the institution.
2. Develop a schedule that will incorporate key leadership topics and provide a sustained experience for participants.
3. Pay careful attention to the opening session as an entry point for building commitment and community in a safe space.
4. Select presenters who are leaders at local, state, and national levels.
5. Invite presenters who are experts in leadership skill topics such as team building and conflict resolution.
6. Select relevant readings that will inspire, challenge, and develop participants' knowledge base.

Chapter Three

Budget

LEARNING GOAL

- Identify options for creating and implementing a cost-effective leadership program.

The importance of developing leaders to meet institutional challenges in times of change is often a touted strategic goal. However, financial constraints are a consideration. Funding has been an issue for community colleges for decades. It is more likely that colleges will support programs that provide a quality, beneficial, and affordable opportunity. A leadership program is cost effective if planners identify key areas where it is possible to use resources wisely. (See Table 3.1 for a sample budget.)

PROGRAM PERSONNEL

A leadership program does not require a full-time person solely dedicated to running the program. Coordinating the leadership program can be a part-time position or one responsibility in the portfolio of a full-time person. A person from human resources or an office of professional development is a reasonable choice for this responsibility. A coordinator could also be a faculty member released from part of a teaching load. Regardless of the choice of coordinator, it is important for this person to spend time becoming familiar with the literature on leadership development.

Whether there is an administrator or faculty member who accepts responsibility for program coordination, it is helpful to have a second person serve as a co-coordinator. Not only does this help divide the responsibilities, it also

Table 3.1. Sample Budget

	Number	Total Amount	% of Budget
Presenters			
Professional Paid	4	$2500	23
Internal Gift	5	$200	2
External Gift	10	$400	4
Food			
Opening Day	2 meals	$750	7
Session Lunches	9	$1800	16
National Speaker Session	1	$600	5
Alumni Luncheon	1	$600	5
Materials			
HBDI	20	$1850	17
Books	20	$800	7
Copyright Reproductions		$500	5
Binders	20	$200	2
Miscellaneous		$300	3
Awards			
Trophies	20	$500	5

Total of budget percentages does not add up to 100 due to rounding.

provides a person with a different perspective and can model collaboration in leadership. At Community College of Philadelphia, a graduate of the Leadership Institute often serves as a co-coordinator. This person is selected based on the leadership qualities demonstrated both in the institution and during his/her participation in the Institute.

It is also helpful if there is a person who provides clerical support as part of his/her current position. While a coordinator can handle clerical responsibilities, having this support enables a greater focus on planning and implementation of the program activities.

PRESENTERS

Engaging both internal and external presenters keeps the program fresh, relevant, and affordable. Using internal presenters for some sessions not only keeps expenses reasonable but also connects institutional leaders to the program and the participants. In turn, participants have the opportunity to learn from senior leaders willing to share their stories and knowledge. Some topics that lend themselves to senior leader presentations include decision making, finances, and grant preparation. Most institutional presenters will accept a small honorarium, gift, or even a thank-you for their contributions.

Faculty presenters are good choices for program sessions for which they have practical expertise. For example, if the program plan includes having participants make presentations on their projects, a faculty member who teaches communications can facilitate a session to provide tips for enhancing the presentations. Faculty who have the credentials and experience in administering and presenting tools like the Myers-Briggs Type Indicator or Herrmann Brain Dominance Instrument® Assessment (HBDI® Assessment) can apply their expertise in the interpretation of such assessments.

An important goal of the leadership program is to provide participants with a local, regional, and national perspective. We can all be so engaged in the day-to-day requirements of a position in an institution that we may not have time to understand how our work fits into a broader context. This will be the case for participants of the leadership program, particularly if their positions do not require interacting with leaders in various departments within or outside the institution.

Presenters who can speak to the local or regional context include the superintendent of the local school district, an educational representative of the mayor's office or governor's office, a representative of the state department of education, a panel of community college presidents in the region, or the president of a partner university.

National presenters may include the CEO or board chair for a national organization like the Association of Community College Trustees, the president or board chair of the American Association of Community Colleges, or the deputy assistant secretary for community colleges. If a national leader will be in the area for a meeting or conference, this is an opportunity to arrange a schedule so that he/she can speak at the college at that time. National leaders will often present pro gratis or for the cost of travel expenses.

Speakers external to the institution are best for topics like conflict resolution or diversity and inclusion. Participants tend to engage more freely in the conversation for such topics if the presenter is not a colleague at the institution. Colleagues from other institutions or consultants may be good resources for those topics. Such speakers receive a modest stipend.

MATERIALS

Common materials for a leadership program are selected books, articles, and an assessment tool. Expenses are minimal for the reading materials, and they provide a context for the program and resources for the topics addressed.

A book representing leadership skills pertinent to the program goals is provided to the participants prior to the start of the program. Reading a leadership book as a group can be a good bonding experience and it creates a jumping-off point for discussion. Questions provided along with the book assist readers in their thinking and analysis of concepts presented. A leadership book also makes an affordable gift for presenters.

Articles help to round out the information provided to participants in specific workshop sessions. Presenters may have specific recommendations for articles that support their presentation. Fees for copying are minimal or none; however, it is important to follow copyright requirements for any materials used.

Leadership style assessments provide insight for participants and coordinators. Some, such as the Myers-Briggs Type Indicator and Herrmann Brain Dominance Instrument® Assessment, require an administration fee. There are free options, however. The VIA Institute's Character Strengths Test (https://www.viacharacter.org/survey/account/register) is one viable example. Participants must register and create a password to take this evidence-based assessment. The 15-minute questionnaire is based on research from positive psychology that emphasizes using one's strengths at work and in life as opposed to concentrating on fixing weaknesses. *Psychology Today* has a free 35-minute test for emotional intelligence (https://www.psychologytoday.com/tests/personality/emotional-intelligence-test). Participants get suggestions for improvement as well as a summary evaluation and graph of their personal results.

HOSPITALITY

Hospitality can be one of the major expenses of the program. Providing breakfast, lunch, or dinner (depending on the time of the sessions) and snacks (for daylong sessions) adds to the sense of investment the institution has in the program and the participants. Partaking in a meal together also enhances community. However, if the budget is tight, providing light refreshments instead of a meal for most or all of the sessions is an option.

The budget may also need to include hospitality for presenters, particularly if they are providing their services at no cost. For example, a session involving a panel of community college presidents may include a lunch with the host president prior to the presentation.

Consider including hospitality for a final celebration for participants. This is a time for participants to share the results of their project work and to reflect publicly on their program experience. Mentors, supervisors, senior leaders, and program alumni are invited. The focus of the event is the accomplishments of the participants, so hospitality can be minimal.

FACILITIES

Having the first meeting off campus as an all-day meeting can be an important way to start the program. A conference room offered by a local partner gets participants out of the usual work environment and signals the importance of the program for the institution. At Community College of Philadelphia, a corporate partner within walking distance of the college has been generous in letting us use their facilities at no cost. A note acknowledging their support of the institution and the initiative is always appreciated. For other meetings, campus meeting rooms meet the needs of the program.

RECOGNITION

Certificates are an inexpensive form of recognition for participants. A senior leader awarding the certificate makes the recognition memorable. At Community College of Philadelphia, we also give out "awards" in addition to certificates. These are simple but elegant glass trophies with the graduate's name and year of participation. This was an added expense, but participants' appreciation made this a reasonable choice for us.

SCHEDULE

After offering the Leadership Institute at Community College of Philadelphia for 10 years, we decided to provide the program every other year as a budget-saving strategy. This change required us to make greater recruitment efforts to avoid an "out of sight, out of mind" reaction. In making this change, we have been successful in sustaining the program with the same level of quality.

SUMMARY OF IDEAS

1. It is possible to run a leadership program in a cost-effective manner.
2. Thoughtful selection of coordinators and internal and external presenters can ensure quality at a low cost.

3. Hospitality and materials can be a major expense but there are ways to minimize the cost.
4. Offering the program every other year can cut the expense for the institution but will require increased efforts for recruitment to sustain program interest.

Chapter Four

Thinking Styles and Team Building

LEARNING GOALS

- Examine the relationship between thinking styles and team building.
- Understand one model for building effective teams.
- Gain insights from one expert on team building.
- Consider some approaches to increase effectiveness of teams.

TEAMS AND THINKING STYLES

Effective teams are a significant component in the success of organizations, including higher education. College presidents face an increasingly complex environment that they cannot handle alone. Building effective teams to handle specific aspects important to the institution frees them up to focus on the areas unique to their positions. Departments across the institution function better when people understand their roles in relation to other team members and can coordinate efforts.

The relationship between thinking styles and team building demands attention and intention. Often, in an effort to reach a goal in a specific time frame imposed by internal or external conditions, a team may not have a chance to develop. The group leader may not take the time to assess the culture of the group, to gain input from the members, or establish a collaborative direction. The momentum found at the outset may not last as comfort and trust dwindle. Building teams takes time, but the effort expended at the outset yields an increased possibility of positive results.

Understanding one's thinking style aids individuals in better understanding the choices and decisions they make for themselves both professionally and personally. Knowing the preferred styles of team members enables a more productive team experience as members can take on those tasks that call on their strengths and thus reach team goals more efficiently and effectively. Especially under pressure, when teams tend to revert to their comfort zones, some team members may take a backseat to stronger voices. It is important at these points to step back a moment to review a team's makeup and recognize the contributions of differing style perspectives. Teams may also decide to add members with a thinking style not represented in the group.

There are various models for determining thinking styles. At Community College of Philadelphia, Leadership Institute teams were initially developed using the Myers-Briggs Type Inventory, a widely used instrument for determining style preference. At the request of Leadership Institute participants in one of our cohorts, we researched another tool, the Herrmann Brain Dominance Instrument® Assessment (HBDI® Assessment), to further inform and understand thinking styles. An outside presenter, the same person who facilitated our team-building session, provided a workshop on the instrument, participants weighed in on its usefulness, and it was decided to use the HBDI® Assessment with future cohorts.

The HBDI® Assessment is based on the position that our mental preferences affect how we process information and communicate with the world. The four thinking preferences presented in a quadrant graphic are: (1) logical and analytical self (A); (2) practical and organized self (B); (3) feeling and relational self (C); and (4) explorer and experimental self (D) (see Figure 4.1).

These preferences may be applied to individuals, groups, and organizations. Although individuals may demonstrate strength in certain thinking preferences, they find that they may also have characteristics of other preferences which are less strong. Knowing this enables individuals to intentionally cultivate weaker preferences or strengthen group composition with a mix of preferences resulting in performance with a whole-brain approach. (See Table 4.1 for Herrmann Whole Brain® Model Key Descriptors of Preferences.)

A 6-year study by DeRidder and Wilcox (1999) examined factors that increase the productivity and efficiency of teams. Using the Whole Brain® Model as the foundation for their work, along with thinking-style data from Herrmann Brain Dominance Instrument® Assessments, their findings included

- Teams that are balanced in terms of thinking preferences are more effective; they consider more options and make better decisions.
- Whole Brained teams were 66% more efficient than homogenous teams.
- 70% or more of the teams were "successful" when Whole Brained vs. 30% or less when not.

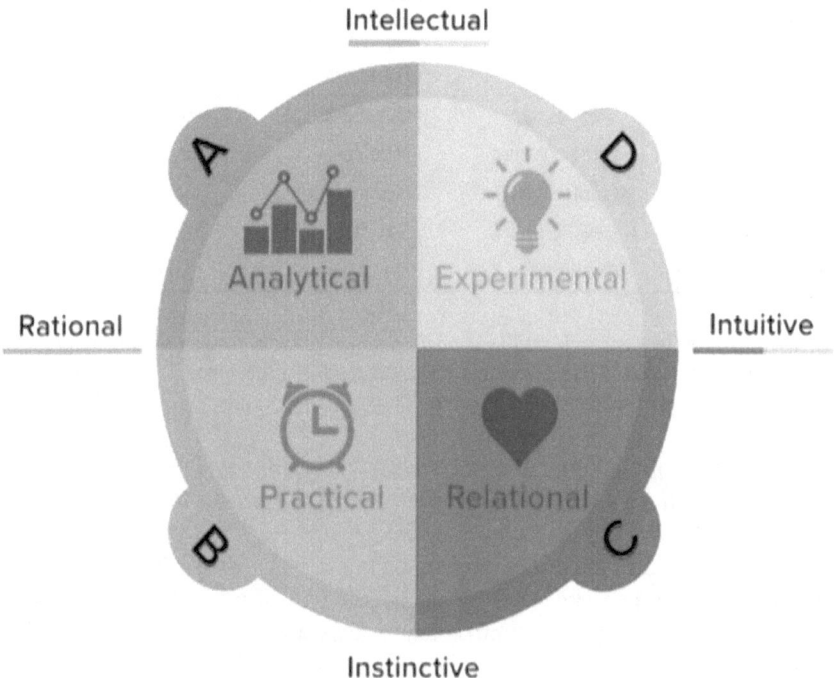

Figure 4.1. Herrmann Whole Brain® Model. The four-color, four-quadrant graphic and Whole Brain® are registered trademarks of Herrmann Global, LLC. © 2016 Herrmann Global, LLC.

It is recommended that the assessment to determine thinking style be completed prior to the start of the program, and that participants receive a comprehensive profile of their results with in-depth interpretation, reference materials, and a visual graphic of their preferences. The graphic also provides a person's preferences when they are under pressure, as noted by the dotted lines. For example, under pressure, a person may tend to be more relational and less experimental. (See Figure 4.2 for Graphic Presentation of Herrmann Brain Dominance® Average Profile.)

Participants particularly like the visual graphic, the accessibility of the descriptors, and the ease of completing the assessment. They also are more attuned to their thinking preferences and those of their teammates. One Community College of Philadelphia participant remarked,

> As we developed our team project, I recognized that my way of thinking and expressing my thoughts would have to shift in order to be a better partner. I tend to think abstractly and had trouble nailing down the best way to execute

Table 4.1. Herrmann Whole Brain® Model Key Descriptors of Four Thinking Preferences

Analytical (A)	Practical (B)	Relational (C)	Experimental (D)
Logical	Sequential	Emotional	Metaphoric
Quantitative	Conservative	Musical	Integrative
Analytical	Controlled	Humanistic	Visual
Technical	Detailed	Expressive	Synthesizing
Factual	Organized	Sensory	Conceptual

our project in a concrete and systematic manner. Careful discussion, planning and project management resulted in a successful project that I feel proud introducing to a wider audience and look forward to working on in the future.

Herrmann International also provides a "Team Ready-for-Action Assessment" tool delineated by thinking preferences for teams to establish their group's composition. For each preference, teams assess to what extent on a scale of 1 to 3 they have the various characteristics of a whole brain. For example, all the data and research we need (A quadrant); clear priorities, a plan, and a timeline (B quadrant); clear understanding of each other's roles and how we interact (C quadrant); new ideas and solutions that challenge the status quo (D quadrant). A "Team Planning Walk-Around" tool serves to periodically monitor their ongoing work. (See www.herrmannsolutions.com for information on these tools.)

INTERVIEW WITH AN EXPERT ON TEAM BUILDING

One of our consistent presenters in Community College of Philadelphia's (CCP) Leadership Institute is Deb Cummins Stellato who assesses participants' thinking styles, both as individuals and as a group, and leads them through team-building exercises in which they gain insights into their approaches to a task and their relationship with others.

Ms. Stellato is the president of Think Good Leadership. Formerly, she served as executive director for Habitat for Humanity of the Lehigh Valley in Pennsylvania. Deb also worked for an internationally known diversity and inclusion firm in the areas of leadership development and new business sales and marketing. As a small business owner, Deb has traveled nationally to develop leadership curricula for emerging leaders and to deliver keynote speeches and programs to various organizations.

Since CCP's first Leadership Institute (LI) in 2002, Deb has inspired LI participants with her energy, enthusiasm, and expertise on thinking styles and team building. Susan Tobia spoke with Deb Cummins Stellato on May 6,

Thinking Styles and Team Building 25

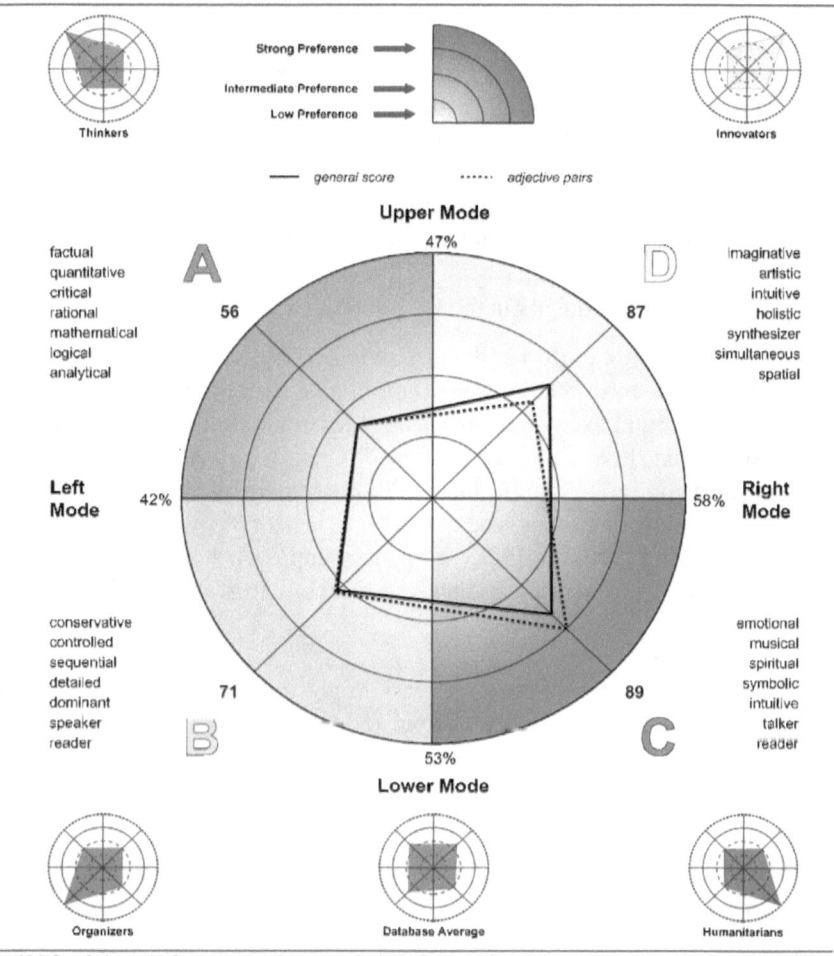

Figure 4.2. Graphic Presentation of Herrmann Brain Dominance® Average Profile.

2016, to tap into her insights on styles and working in teams from the vantage point of her work with various organizations and specifically from her work with the Leadership Institute. The interview has been edited for length and clarity.

Susan: What do you consider the most important aspects of team building for leaders in higher education?

Deb: The approach I take is grounded in Familiarity, Comfort and Trust (FCT). I learned it working in a diversity and inclusion company. It's a good way to look at the evolution of a team. Getting to trust is a journey. The work that I do for CCP's Leadership Institute is to move the participants quickly along the continuum of FCT. For a group that is so diverse every year—that may or may not have that much in common—it is important to get to a place of sharing and trust early on. I am always thinking of that approach when I work with a group and looking at the authenticity of those three components.

S: Can you say a bit more about the FCT approach?

D: The Familiarity, Comfort and Trust approach is essentially a way to look at and build authentic relationships. Familiarity happens when we initially meet each other and exchange introductory information like, "Where do you live?" or "What do you do for a living?" Once we have spent time with people, we begin to feel comfortable with them; perhaps we even exchange more personal information at a deeper level. It is here that we see our authentic self emerging. Trust is tricky as people approach it differently. Some automatically trust others immediately; for others, trust is earned over time through actions.

S: That is why we started our first session, not only with you, but also off campus for a whole day because we wanted the participants to build a community of trust. In fact, if anyone said they would miss the first session or who showed up late, we would ask them to defer their participation in the Institute because it was so critical to establish a community of trust.

D: And for this group to effectively deliver their projects, you also had to have the conversation about style pretty quickly. Whether we used the Myers-Briggs Type Inventory or the Herrmann Brain Dominance Instrument® Assessment (HBDI® Assessment), they were able to talk about their styles, to be transparent, and then we did some practical application with them to ask about their anticipated challenges and opportunities and how they planned to manage them. That was right from the get-go. Sometimes you let a group dance around those issues, but we did not let the group do this with the structure that we had.

S: And how important is safety to building that trust?

D: In the LI, I have always been aware of that component because of the diversity of the groups. There is in some ways a power structure because you have all the components of an academic environment—faculty, administrators, senior-level people, people who are new. The playing field was not equal for everybody who came in. There may have been a disparity in their salaries, in their education. That could be trouble because if you don't work on building a trusting community, you risk a power struggle the whole time you're together.

S: What models have you found effective in determining thinking styles?

D: The Whole Brain® Model exemplified in the HBDI® Assessment has worked for me in working in a diversity and inclusion space in approaching relationships. It is a way of looking at leadership and the importance of diverse teams and how you can capitalize on that relationship.

Utilizing a whole-brain thinking model in leadership development enables the presenter to accelerate the speed of FCT with program participants. The HBDI® Assessment provides safe language that enables individuals to speak freely about their strengths and weaknesses in a healthy environment. It is amazing to see how using this approach builds a depth of relationship that is generally not possible in a first meeting.

Initially in the LI, we started with the Myers-Briggs which is a very well documented, popular model. What we found was that the Whole Brain® Model was a bit more robust with more data and scientific contributions. It acknowledged in a deeper way those diverse thinking styles. You kind of got to similar places but with a better tool, I think.

S: The HBDI® Assessment was easier; you could simply glance at the graphic to see where you were. It was actually one of the LI teams that researched the HBDI® Assessment and pressed us to have you back because they wanted more information about their styles.

D: In my work, I always think it's important to consider the "stick factor." You may come in and drop your pixie dust, but the group has to be able to apply the model, to actually use it, especially when there is conflict. Baking in a checkpoint such as Herrmann International's "Team Planning Walk-Around" is something I would definitely encourage those building leadership programs to implement.

S: The HBDI® Assessment gave people an awareness both of their own styles (which was often a surprise) and the styles of their team members. This awareness was critical.

D: That's the whole emotional intelligence theory. People who have good emotional intelligence don't even think of it as a skill set, but often it might be the first time for some that they are looking at themselves in the mirror and taking accountability for who they are.

People who join the LI already have an idea that they want to be leaders and you often find them butting heads because they're used to taking the lead. So helping them to think about their thinking styles and to be aware of them and the styles of others is especially important.

S: In your years of experience in working with leadership programs, what stands out for you as one of the most important takeaways about thinking style and its impact on the effectiveness of teams/leaders?

D: I am a systems thinker. I like taking a quick picture of what your culture is going to look like. What's been interesting about working with the LI is that each group has had a different culture and that was reflected in what that Whole Brain® Model looked like. I remember one year where there was a predominance of English faculty and there was a different vibe.

When you look at any of these assessment inventories, not just for individuals but the group, you see a snapshot of the culture from day one and you get a good sense of their strengths and opportunities, and that enables you to look at curriculum and projects differently and to have a framework for their success moving forward. And this culture has other cultures embedded in it as people bring their cultures with them.

CCP is a huge place and there are stereotypes and biases as to what it means to be in different parts of that world. The inclusivity of the program is really the beauty of the program as people from various parts of the college have the opportunity to participate. In a lot of leadership programs, you must be at a certain level or have a certain amount of experience. What's cool about the LI is that you have really opened it up, and providing a context and the tools for them to navigate the different cultures has been really helpful.

S: A predominant comment from participants is that they would never have gotten to know people in the LI who are from various parts of the college. And in many cases, it helped their own work as it gave them resources—people they could call upon to enrich their work. They feel more a part of the whole college.

D: The whole silo effect is what higher education often falls into. So this is an opportunity to not only work out of individual department silos but also the bigger silos such as academic or administration. When people have an opportunity to share different perspectives over a period of time, they often find they have more things in common than expected and feel more comfortable working across units. The FCT approach is especially effective in facilitating this.

S: When teams don't work well, is there a usual suspect that you explore in helping the team get back on track?

D: I do really believe that there are people who are toxic in organizations, and it can be quite powerful to identify that behavior and understand how it affects the team. As a leader, you have the choice as to how to deal with it. My approach is to try to rescue people who are toxic—coach them and try to change them—learn about them and try to be flexible with my own leadership style.

For example, in one of the LI groups there was a participant who came in the door with an attitude that wasn't congruent with what was happening, and the coordinators picked up on that and addressed it before it became a bigger problem. I totally believe that people are coachable, and as a leader it is your job to coach them to help them bring out their best assets. And you also have to be honest in your assessment as to if it's a behavior you can continue to tolerate. When you risk losing other staff members, it's up to the leader to make the hard decisions.

S: As coordinators, when contentious issues came up in team projects, we would meet with the team to work it through, and often people would swallow their own egos to get through it and complete the project because they realized the team was more important than the individuals at that point. Sometimes there were teammates going in different directions that made it tough, but to their credit, they didn't quit.

D: I think groups will always have that possibility. One thing you always have to be aware of as a leader is where your energy goes. So if you follow the 80/20 rule and you're spending 80% of your energy in trying to fix the team dynamic to get to the goal, that's exhausting and you end up producing 20% results. You can't let it suck the life out of you. Sometimes it just isn't the right fit.

S: What insights have you gained over time as you have worked with leadership programs?

D: I've worked on college campuses where participants have worked closely together as a team and 30 years later they have continued their relationships with one another, and so there is really something about relationships. They have committed to the group and they have made a commitment to themselves to grow and to move outside their comfort zones which is critical.

They also develop, especially with a yearlong program, an appreciation for the institution that is making the commitment to them. That has great value for things like retention and changing perceptions for the positive. And you hope there is a trickle effect where people take what they are learning back to their departments, to the people they mentor or teach. What's so magical about these experiences is that trickle effect and how much a difference it can make in what's going on in an organization.

S: What important changes have you made?

D: Each group is so unique that the biggest mindset I've had in working with groups is to maintain my role as a facilitator, which is more important than the training role. The training role is more content related, while facilitation is more listening to understand where the group is functioning, which is the harder and more important part. The content doesn't change all that much, and I use the tools dictated by my certification process. I'm always reminded with these groups not to have expectations and not to compare them from year to year and not to make any assumptions. So keeping my eye on the facilitation is more important, and the mindset helps to ensure that practice.

ENSURING SUCCESSFUL TEAMS

Some teams are more successful than others, and anyone who has been a member of a team can testify to this. But why? Pentland and his researchers at MIT's Human Dynamics Laboratory sought to answer this question. Examining data from many similar teams with varying performance, they found that a team's communication patterns were key to its success, as important as intelligence, personality, and talent combined. They found that successful teams shared several defining characteristics:

1. Everyone on the team talks and listens in roughly equal measure, keeping contributions short and sweet.
2. Members face one another, and their conversations and gestures are energetic.
3. Members connect directly with one another—not just with the team leader.
4. Members carry on back-channel or side conversations within the team.
5. Members periodically break, go exploring outside the team, and bring information back. (Pentland, 2012)

If team members are aware of these characteristics, they can make adjustments as necessary to achieve a more successfully functioning team.

Managing a group's emotional intelligence is another avenue for ensuring a successful team experience. Druskat and Wolff (2001) define a group's emotional intelligence as a combination of self-management and relational skills. Their research found that the essential conditions for a group's effectiveness were mutual trust, a sense of group identity, and a sense of group efficacy. Cultivating these conditions, which are built on an understanding of individual emotions and the emotions of others within the team, led to greater participation and collaboration among members. This resulted in positive group outcomes.

Druskat and Wolff offer suggestions for assisting groups in establishing norms that create awareness of emotions and norms that help regulate emotions. For example, group norms for creating awareness of emotions include

- acknowledging and discussing group moods,
- allowing members to call for a "process" check,
- communicating a sense of what is transpiring in the team, and
- seeking feedback from others.

Group norms that help regulate emotions include

- creating fun ways to acknowledge and relieve tension,
- reminding members of the group's mission,
- focusing on what the group can control, and
- taking the initiative to understand and get what the group needs to be effective.

Norms can be introduced by leadership program coordinators, group members, or outside presenters. The imperative is to cultivate emotionally intelligent teams that work to achieve positive outcomes.

LESSONS FROM COMMUNITY COLLEGE OF PHILADELPHIA (CCP)

One approach that CCP offered for increasing the success of teams in the discussion context is Edward de Bono's Six Thinking Hats method. De Bono (1999) posits that a typical Western-style meeting encourages dualistic thinking, one side vs. the other. Certain people may dominate the discussion while others are hesitant to express their ideas or true feelings. Different people consider different issues from different viewpoints, and meetings get bogged down in politics, personalities, and power plays. Too much is happening at once, and there is no sense of order in trying to reach a resolution. Sound familiar?

De Bono, a psychologist, physician, and writer, was critical of this type of thinking and came up with a method that changes the structure of group discussion. His Six Thinking Hats method offers a process for unscrambling a group's thinking. Called parallel thinking, everyone in the group looks at the same issue, at the same time with a specific lens (hat). The group leader keeps members thinking under the direction of that hat and allows a switch to other lenses (hats) throughout the discussion to encourage reflective problem solving rather than dualistic thinking.

De Bono used colors for the hats (thinking caps) to make it easy to remember the kind of thinking the group is engaged in at any given moment. (See Appendix J for a description of the Six Thinking Hats and Appendix K for keys to a successful Six Thinking Hats session.)

CCP participants found this approach intriguing and noted some similarities to the HBDI® Assessment styles of thinking. For example, the Relational thinking preference and the Red hat both include an emotional focus. Comments made by participants from various cohorts in terms of how they might use the Six Hats approach in their Leadership Institute teams or in their departments include

- I love it for its usefulness in generating ideas and conversation while staying on track!
- My department is very red hat. Being able to acknowledge that and have an organized method to move forward will be useful.
- I can see using this in the classroom with group projects.
- It would help establish an even playing field when looking at an issue and allow for more focused debate.

SUMMARY OF IDEAS

1. Understanding one's thinking style and the styles of other group members enables a more productive team experience.
2. Using a model such as the Herrmann Brain Dominance Instrument® Assessment helps build teams with diverse thinking preferences, which contributes to a whole-brain approach.
3. Moving a cohort along a Familiarity, Comfort and Trust continuum is important in establishing an inclusive culture that recognizes the strengths of its diversity.
4. Providing opportunities early on for participants to share their thinking styles with one another opens up meaningful dialogue and facilitates a community of trust.
5. A team's communication patterns are one of the most critical elements in its effectiveness.
6. Managing a group's emotional intelligence serves to cultivate trust, group identity, and group efficacy.
7. Using an approach such as the Six Thinking Hats to facilitate a group discussion keeps the members focused while helping them to entertain diverse perspectives in a structured way.

Chapter Five

Team Projects

LEARNING GOALS

- Recognize the benefits of team projects.
- Understand one theoretical model for developing effective teams.
- Gain ideas in the use of team projects in leadership development.

BENEFITS OF TEAM PROJECTS

An essential component of the Leadership Institute at Community College of Philadelphia (CCP) is the completion of a project of benefit to the college community and of interest to the participants. In their study of Grow Your Own (GYO) programs, Reille and Kezar (2010) note that although team projects were recognized as valuable, these were rarely included in the GYO programs due to the potentially overwhelming time and effort required of participants. At CCP, we felt that the benefits outweighed these potential challenges and were critical for learning as part of the Institute experience and beyond.

A recommended goal is to ensure a diverse experience for the project teams. Building relationships in which people trust one another and are open to learning from different perspectives leads to positive change. In the process of forming project teams, one should be intentional about mixing styles, backgrounds of experience, and organizational positions. It is human nature to gravitate toward others who are "like" us, so the team formation process should emphasize diverse college representation. Having input from team members representing different aspects of the organization, offering a diversity of ideas and experiences, and committed to working as a team can yield more powerful outcomes.

Teams are also beneficial in awakening members to goals and values from an institutional viewpoint. It is easy, especially in larger organizations, to stay isolated within a particular department without any meaningful connection to the organization as a whole. A person may be accomplishing positive outcomes for that department but at the same time be unaware of the impact on other parts of the organization. Further, she may not have knowledge that similar outcomes are being achieved by other departments that could further inform her work, and she may miss the opportunity to learn from others' mistakes.

This silo mentality has often been cited as a cause for lack of institutional communication and collaboration resulting in decreased efficiency and effectiveness (Stone, 2004). Cilliers and Greyvenstein (2012) found the silo mentality to be the tip of the iceberg with the largest effect occurring below the surface in unconscious behaviors that influenced teams negatively, making boundary crossing difficult.

As one Leadership Institute participant at CCP described her experience,

> ... I often find myself turning my energy inward toward my classes and my department. In part, I do this because it seems so difficult to get anything done on an institutional level.... However, it is also incredibly rewarding when you do get a project completed. I feel that the knowledge I gained from my teammates and from this project will encourage me to become more institutionally active and will give me more confidence to deal with institutional issues in the future.

STEPS TO DEVELOPING EFFECTIVE PROJECT TEAMS — LESSONS FROM COMMUNITY COLLEGE OF PHILADELPHIA

Research abounds on developing and managing teams to successfully meet goals of organizations, both small and large. One model that fit the goals and processes for Community College of Philadelphia's Leadership Institute is Hackman's Five Factor Model, an evidence-based model for team effectiveness. Hackman posits that the conventional approach is to focus on the team leader as the major influence on team effectiveness. A more unconventional model is to attribute performance of team members, whether they are succeeding or failing, as one of the major influences on a group's interaction processes. Both approaches attribute causality to either the leader or the team members. As an alternative, Hackman suggests a focus on the structural and contextual conditions under which groups perform over time. Those conditions, which when present increase team effectiveness, are

1. Being a Real Team: Members have a shared task; team boundaries exist for membership; and the membership is stable.

2. Compelling Direction: Team has clear goals, which are both challenging and consequential.
3. Enabling Structure: Task, composition, and norms of conduct enable rather than impede the team's work.
4. Supportive Context: Teams are rewarded for their work; members have opportunity to develop skills; and teams have access to information and other resources to be successful.
5. Expert Coaching and Mentoring: Teams are provided with resource people who have expertise in the team's task and serve to offer advice that allows for consideration without being too directive.

(Hackman, 2004)

Step 1: Creating Diverse Teams

At Community College of Philadelphia, we had a debate in the first year of the program as to whether we should require participants to work in project teams and whether we should choose the teams or allow participants to choose their own. Eventually we compromised and gave participants the option of working either alone or as part of a team, and allowing those who chose to work in teams to self-select their teams. The results were that five teams of varying size were formed and five participants chose to pursue individual projects.

We made several observations based on this structure. Participants who were part of a team were better connected to the entire group as well as to their teams, and the group projects were generally more ambitious than individual projects. However, our self-selected teams tended to be homogeneous. In four of the groups, faculty teamed with faculty, and administrators teamed with administrators. The one mixed group consisted of faculty and staff (hourly workers). Clearly, self-selected teams and individual projects were not serving to forge the kinds of connections among different areas of the college we wanted to see, and participants were not gaining the experience of working with people who have different styles and perspectives.

From then on, we decided not only to require a team project but to assign participants to teams based on factors such as different thinking styles, employee categories, race, gender, and levels of expertise (based on program applications). There was some initial anxiety in doing this, but we felt that the experience gained by working in a diverse group with people from across the college would push participants to acquire those relationship skills, which are such an important part of leadership, and to practice other skills such as conflict resolution and effective decision making, which are emphasized in the second half of the program.

As Rock and Grant (2016) point out, diverse teams are more likely to question biases, reexamine facts, and hold each other to the team's objectives. In the context of moving their projects forward, close interactions with team members and other colleagues challenge participants to be more aware of their own habits of mind and ways of interacting with others; be more conscious and appreciative of others' differences; communicate more effectively; learn more about the organizational culture at the college; acquire better navigational skills; and solve problems collaboratively. Not only are the projects generally more substantial in breadth and depth, but participants also gain insights about themselves which they can apply in their home departments.

A participant in CCP's Institute commented that if she had not been assigned to a project team, she wouldn't have had such a rich experience in which she learned not only about other people's jobs but also how different approaches to a problem could enlighten her own thinking. She felt compelled to reexamine her assumptions about people and her natural responses to problem solving and to ask questions of her team members that in turn informed her work in venues outside of the Leadership Institute. One team struggled with their differences in approach but worked through the barriers to successfully complete their project. This was an equally valuable learning experience and highlighted the challenges that often arise in institutions which may have competing agendas. One team member remarked,

> There were many challenges with personalities, scheduling and who was the boss and who were the followers. After many struggles and many interventions, we have come out with something that I am so proud of. . . . So many times, I came close to quitting this team and walking away from something that in the end has changed my life forever. I am so glad there were people who changed my mind, both on my team and off.

At CCP, project teams are intentionally mixed according to thinking styles established through the Herrmann Brain Dominance Instrument® Assessment which participants take online prior to the Institute. The model was developed by Ned Herrmann, a physicist by training, while head of Management Development at General Electric in the early 1980s. It is based on a holistic, whole-brain thinking model. Coordinators use the results to compose the project teams with the goal of "creating" a whole brain (see Chapter 4 for further details).

As previously noted, project teams also include members who represent different areas within the college and bring to the table different skills, strengths, perspectives, and experiences. The teams are a great opportunity to forge working relationships among colleagues who would not ordinarily get the chance to work together. As one participant at CCP put it,

> This project served to help me make everything I learned in the Leadership Institute real including working in a team, planning and implementing a pro-

ject, and working within a complex system of colleagues and leaders. I wanted to get to know more about how the other offices worked and I did. I wanted to learn how to build bridges for integrated projects and I did. I wanted to learn how to bring innovation into a system that is so large with so many responsibilities that it should resist it, but the system had a process for changing and I was able to observe and be a part of it.

Step 2: Providing Structure and Support

A primary goal of the project is to raise awareness of larger higher educational issues in relation to institutional goals and to develop new and effective ways to work together to achieve them. A second major goal is for participants to further develop leadership abilities on an experiential level. Thus, participants are encouraged to take a broad perspective on issues relevant to the projects by making use of insights gained from local, state, and national trends impacting the college and the larger community. These perspectives are developed in the first part of the program.

Participants are encouraged to make use of already existing institutional research relevant to their projects and are also encouraged to engage in institutional research as needed. Likewise, they are invited to draw on their increased understanding of the nature of leadership and of self in relation to others and to develop improved strategies for navigating the complexities of one's organizational culture and solving problems collaboratively.

The project teams are formed in the early part of the Institute and membership is stable throughout the program. Ground rules developed by the entire Institute cohort at the first meeting apply to the project teams as well. This ensures that everyone feels comfortable within the group and is free to express, question, and openly discuss ideas about the projects as they evolve.

In the first few years of the program at CCP, participants were given a great deal of latitude regarding project topics. They were told simply that the projects had to be of interest to themselves and of benefit to the college community. At the suggestion of participants who requested more structure with the projects, we decided to tie the projects more concretely to institutional goals by identifying a specific theme related to an important aspect of our strategic plan, such as improving retention and persistence.

We developed a project directive and a project overview guide to assist participants in defining and implementing their projects. (See Appendix L for a sample project directive and Appendix M for the project overview guide.) We also provided closer feedback in the early stages of project proposals which generated more focused and more realistic projects.

Participants from one CCP cohort commented that there was not a strong connection between their project work and the seminar sessions. Thus, we intentionally incorporated issues confronted by project teams into our presentation discussions. For example, such issues as "gaining consensus" and the "politics of organizations" were explicitly addressed in conflict-resolution and decision-making sessions.

Scope of the Projects

It is important to limit the scope of the projects so that they can be accomplished during the year or at a maximum in the subsequent year. Participants tend to dream big, which is admirable, but they should be directed to establish goals which are achievable in the time they have together. A caution for extending the deadline is the need for consistent follow-up with the team beyond the end date of the program to provide assistance as needed and to assure they are on task to complete. Sometimes the pursuit of an achievable goal means taking the project in a different direction than initially planned. As one team member at CCP commented,

> Working on this project has made me realize how the accomplishment of a project does not happen in a "straight line." Initial ideas branch off into even newer ideas. One change in a project can lead to other unanticipated changes. I think the challenge for a leader is to move effectively with change. The process of our project is very much like what happens to leaders in the world on a daily basis. Unexpected things do happen. In these situations, some may become paralyzed and others will find a way to move forward. I am proud to be a member of a group who decided to regroup, examine our options, and move forward with accomplishing our goal in a different way.

At CCP, we also provided more support throughout the year, enabling team members to spend more time together as well as with coordinators. As noted by Reille and Kezar (2010), the time and effort required to include projects in leadership programs was a prime reason for excluding them. The projects required extra time in already busy schedules for participants, so one way to address this was to adapt the monthly Institute schedule to build in more project time as well as scheduled time with coordinators outside of the monthly meetings. Although a first strategy may be to allow teams to work out any struggles on their own, at times a team may experience a minor meltdown, and coordinators should respond by engaging the team in facilitated problem solving.

Financial Support

The Leadership Institute at CCP provides no financial support for projects, but participants are encouraged to apply for mini-grants through the College Foundation. For example, one of CCP's first-year teams won a grant to initiate an Alumni Speaker Series. The Alumni Affairs person from Institutional Advancement and the Career Services person worked together to bring alumni back to the campus to speak with undergraduates about their careers and help to connect them to their future professions. Articles were then written about the alumni for the alumni newsletter, helping to reconnect them to the college.

Other projects were indirectly funded through departments that decided to implement project ideas consonant with their existing goals. (See textbox 5.1 for sample of department supported projects.)

SAMPLE OF PROJECTS SUPPORTED THROUGH DEPARTMENTS

The *Majors Fair* empowered undecided students to make better choices by increasing their awareness of options regarding majors, programs, degrees, and transfer opportunities.

The *Student Portal Tutorial Project* provided a tutorial for students on how to use the new student portal and utilize the resources available to them.

The *Library Services Video Project* offered a student-centered video to help students navigate the library and all its resources.

The *CCP Alternative Spring Break* provided a domestic service-learning project to be held during the college's spring break. Students and chaperones traveled to a designated site and assisted in the construction of a building or other community service as needed.

Support From the Wider Community

Halfway through the year, during CCP's Professional Development Week, the Leadership Institute project teams present their project proposals to members of the college community for questions and feedback. (See Appendix N for a sample invitation.) They have the advantage of presenting their ideas before an audience with expertise and experience in areas relevant to the various proposals, thus enabling Institute participants to make appropriate adjustments.

Feedback from invited guests, including mentors, has proved invaluable in helping participants to define the scope of the projects more carefully and delineate steps to completion, to clarify logistics and institutional context, as well as to identify resources not yet considered. Audience members have also helped teams become aware of flaws or weaknesses in their projects. For example, one team was essentially pursuing two separate projects and had not succeeded in unifying its efforts. Some team members were aware of the problem but had not been able to address it. When audience members kept insisting that there were two projects, the whole team was finally able to hear it and resolve the problem.

Audience members also provide written feedback to participants with specific suggestions as well as encouragement and constructive criticism. (See Appendix O for a presentation feedback form.) The written feedback is gathered and presented to each team which has the option of revising its project. In most cases, the feedback received has resulted in stronger, more relevant projects. They also have been more likely to receive support for incorporation within the relevant departmental structure. An added benefit of this activity is that it heightens awareness of the Institute and encourages support among members of the college community.

Each project team presents an oral final report at the completion of the Leadership Institute to colleagues, mentors, and other invited guests. (See Appendix P for final report specs.) This session serves to showcase the results of the team efforts, to demonstrate the utilization of institutional feedback, to afford practice of presentation skills in a larger arena, and to highlight new leadership. Several of the projects have been implemented at CCP or have contributed to the implementation of similar efforts, including the *Majors Fair*, *VetConnect*, *Student Portal Tutorial*, *Library Services Video*, *Academic Checkup*, *Alternative Spring Break*, *Sound Off*, and *Steps on the Path*. (See Appendix Q for a summary of these projects and others completed.) Even if a project is not implemented, it is a success if participants learn from their experiences.

Step 3: Mentoring/Coaching

In their study of Grow Your Own programs, Reille and Kezar (2010) note that although there is wide agreement on the importance of mentoring, very few programs include mentors because of the difficulty in coordination and the commitment required. However, at CCP, we felt the inclusion of mentors was a worthy effort, so in the third year of the Leadership Institute, we added mentors as a resource to the project teams.

Mentors, who are often senior leaders in the institution, have proven to be a valuable resource to participants for several reasons. First, as senior leaders, they provide broad institutional knowledge, and they can lessen the potential for participants to face turf battles within a complex hierarchy, paving the way to work with others in areas under their supervision. Second, mentors are in a position to quickly identify the person or persons with some stake in the project topic and enlist their support. Third, mentors have expertise related to the specific project topic. They meet with the members of the project team—as the need arises and as their schedule allows—to provide practical advice to aid in the completion of the project and to provide insights and ideas regarding assessing its impact and in sustaining it beyond the

Leadership Institute year. Finally, mentors provide participants with opportunities to work with others across the college community, which supports the Institute's effort to broaden the perspectives of participants beyond their individual departments.

One CCP participant commented that in the planning stages of her team's project, they did not consider the legal ramifications the project could have for the college. "Being conscious of how a project may affect the college has been beneficial because it changes one's understanding of why some things that may seem like good projects or policies cannot be instituted at the college."

An important responsibility of the coordinators is to select mentors who have a genuine interest in the respective projects. That interest ensures their investment of time and commitment. It is important to communicate clearly with prospective mentors about the purpose of their contribution and the expectations. Mentors are invited to participate in working sessions, especially in the second half of the program, to afford a common place and time for collaboration and feedback. At CCP, we learned that mentors also benefit as they often work with people who may not fall directly under their supervision and appreciate the fresh ideas that participants bring to the projects, or, as Lambert (2015) points out, challenge established ways of thinking and doing. (See Appendix R for a sample mentor request letter.)

TAKEAWAYS FROM LEADERSHIP INSTITUTE PARTICIPANTS

Comments made by participants from various cohorts to the question, "What did you learn from your participation in the team projects?" include

- I learned the value of pooling talents and having team members challenge each other.
- I learned not to stay within my professional comfort zone.
- Good team work is knowing what strengths a person will be able to contribute to a project to make sure it is done well.
- Communication must be at the core. If not, the work will be completed, but a unit connection will never occur.
- I have increased my ability to listen more attentively and exercise patience.
- Someone or some department should be identified as a "champion" of the project for it to succeed.
- I am accustomed to doing things myself, so it was a nice change to rely on others for their knowledge, resources, insights, and perceptions.
- I learned that people have very different ideas of what are the "best" ways to proceed. I learned not to take things so personally and that those whom

I oppose one day can end up being a great ally the next, as long as it's not personal but about the task at hand.
- I learned a lot about my limitations. I worked well in a team, but I did not necessarily feel as though I was a complete leader. I very much looked up to one teammate who displayed to me many of the ideal characteristics of a leader. I will continue to attempt to emulate her leadership skills.
- I learned to step back and stop trying to take over the project. Once I did this, other team members commented that they felt more a part of the team.
- I learned to connect with people from different parts of the college and became much more aware of the importance of gaining their support.

SUMMARY OF IDEAS

1. Invest in team projects to expand leadership experiences and broaden institutional perspectives.
2. Create diverse project teams that are stable throughout the program.
3. Identify a tool such as the Herrmann Brain Dominance Instrument® Assessment to diversify teams by thinking preferences.
4. Help teams identify projects that are consequential and can be accomplished within the program year to increase motivation and help participants set realistic goals.
5. Provide feedback about projects from the community beyond the cohort.
6. Offer mentoring support and access to resources to enrich the team project experience.

Part II

Key Leadership Content Areas

Chapter Six

Conflict Resolution

LEARNING GOALS

- Understand basic, evidence-based information about conflict resolution in a work environment.
- Gain insights from one expert on conflict resolution.
- Learn some techniques and resources for preventing and managing conflict.

Conflict in organizations is inevitable. That fact makes conflict resolution an important topic for a leadership program. Goals for a presentation on conflict resolution should include making sure participants know leaders have responsibility for managing conflict even though it may be uncomfortable, understanding how people's mindsets influence how they deal with conflict, and gaining awareness of techniques that may help resolve conflicts.

Conflicts that arise in organizations include those that are interpersonal (conflicts between two or more persons or groups), task related (conflicts over what to do), and process oriented (conflicts over how to accomplish something). The relationship between the parties in a conflict also affects the interaction. Conflicts between peers are different from conflicts between subordinates and supervisors. Regardless of the underlying issue, a leader who does not manage conflict well risks having differences escalate into bigger, more challenging issues. Conflict can be a positive experience or at least have a positive outcome if leaders learn how to think and act in relation to disagreements.

Oore, Leiter, and LeBlanc (2015) identify four individual factors associated with better outcomes in a conflict: cognitive flexibility, a balance of "self" and "other" focus, emotional regulation, and person-conflict fit. Cognitive flexibility is the ability to see or feel an experience from the perspective of another. A leader will encounter different perspectives, personalities, and ideas that may conflict with each other. The ability to understand multiple views is an important skill for a leader, particularly as work environments become more diverse (Prause & Mujtaba, 2015).

Being able to understand multiple perspectives does not mean making the views of others more important than a self-focus. This is particularly the case for conflict between peers. Putting the perspective or feelings of another ahead of one's own in order to get along can be an avoidance mechanism that leads to resentment or a resurfacing of the conflict later. A balance of "self" and "other" focus can bring the right level of effort to creating a positive resolution.

The ability to regulate emotion is a third characteristic associated with more successful conflict resolution. Emotional regulation involves intentionally managing negative emotions. The ability to keep emotions like anger under control can help focus energy on solving a problem in a constructive way.

An appreciation for person-conflict fit is the last variable. People have different preferred styles for dealing with conflict. A style that may be successful in one situation may be ineffective in another. For example, agreeing to disagree may be effective for a minor conflict but is not likely to be a good fit for a significant issue that requires a decision. The college culture may influence person-conflict fit. Some cultures encourage people to openly discuss differences. That culture may be uncomfortable for people who are not used to dealing with conflict in that fashion. People who are adept at modifying their style to the situation or to accommodate the style of the other person may more often be able to achieve person-conflict fit.

There are many ways to approach a presentation on conflict resolution. The approach ultimately will depend on the background of the presenter. An external presenter is a good choice for this topic. Though people in the institution may be experienced and skilled in resolving conflicts, an external person brings the benefit of a person who is not associated with any internal disputes, past or present.

INTERVIEW WITH AN EXPERT ON CONFLICT RESOLUTION

The Leadership Institute at Community College of Philadelphia chose psychologist Dr. Thomas A. Gordon as the presenter on this topic. Dr. Gordon is the founder and principal of TAGA Consulting. He emphasizes systems thinking, effective communication, and understanding of human dynamics in his approach. He has been a coach and consultant to senior leadership internationally as well as serving as a faculty member and psychotherapist.

Dr. Gordon's popularity with the participants resulted in our engaging him to present on conflict resolution for the last 6 years of the program. Susan Tobia interviewed Dr. Gordon on May 12, 2017. The interview has been edited for length and clarity.

Susan: In the Leadership Institute, one reason we form groups that are diverse in thinking style is to avoid situations in which group members choose comfort and select to be with people who are like-minded. Rather, we want them to experience situations in which they feel somewhat uncomfortable in hopes that they grow from those experiences.

Thomas: You're deliberately deploying people to honor diversity. Imagine if the United States practiced that with all the diversity we have. If we deliberately configured and deployed and honored and reinforced diversity, we'd harvest on the other end greater stimulation, learning, discovery, innovation, productivity, and development. Now with it you'd expect some conflict because we're not clones of each other's life exposures, so we'd have to have people who are skillful enough and prepared to work with diversity, to be curious and interested in conflict, and not to view it as an enemy but an inevitable by-product of human complexity interdependently aligned. Human beings can't be involved with each other without thinking and bringing their exposures to situations, so you're going to have this complexity. Rather than label conflict as bad or good, which is a binary trap you can get stuck in, let's label it as inevitable human complexity. Let's study the way it showed up and let's see if we can bring order from this complexity that advances the center—the mission in our lives.

S: So the conflict becomes a catalyst.

T: A conflict becomes a catalyst and a challenge, so now we go from context, culture, and connection to challenges that come with human beings working and living together. From those challenges, we now want to look at choices we can make.

S: You come in at a point in the Institute at which participants have been working on their project teams and there may have been some conflicts that have arisen. It's an opportune time for them to put into practice the insights they gain from the conflict-resolution process.

T: My job is to get them comfortable enough so they don't practice embarrassment thinking and try to hide the conflicts. Knowing the inside partners (program coordinators) and having some knowledge about any conflicts ahead of time gives me an edge. Even if they try to hide, I can do more things to gently invite them to be authentic.

S: In your years of experience in working with leadership programs, what insights stand out to you related to addressing conflict resolution and its impact on the effectiveness of developing leaders?

T: I often assume that there are some distortions of the thinking about the concept of conflict and that probably people have had some negative, painful experiences with conflict. I come in with the assumption that I may have to expand people's thinking about the concept. That distorted thinking may apply to diversity, teaming, racism, etc. A lot of things could have restricted people's thinking, so part of my job is to shine light.

I also come in with the concept of energy in mind, that people do care about something. I want to know what people love or care about. That gives you a chance to be multilingual with them. If you know something that builds for them a sense of positive energy, you might be able to start on a common ground at the level of deepest values. Ideally, you want to speak to them and connect with things they care about so you're not 10,000 feet in the air with abstractions or trying to fix a problem that hasn't spoken to their core need.

So I usually think about light and guidance because there could be some distortions or confusions, and I'm interested in what energizes them. I come in a little bit early in the session and try to hear what's on their minds as they're discussing things: Who talks and who doesn't, who interrupts somebody, and who listens while a point is made. What is their point? What is it that they're animated about? In some sessions, I start off listening and it becomes almost a seamless transition into me being the speaker. I can say, "Given the scenario X and your response Y, have you thought about Z?" Now I'm into what energizes them. From that I can come back to the idea that life is about energy. If it's living, it's changing, it's growing, it's developing. You're just telling me a little about your energy. Now we're at the center of our discussion. Life is about embedded and interdependent systems, small and large.

S: Are there changes/adjustments you have made in your facilitation of groups on the topic of conflict resolution that might be helpful to others?

T: I've seen people go more toward the concrete techniques first, delivered by PowerPoint or delivered in a crisp, efficient manner. The assumption is first that people are asking for it and second that people do need it because not everyone can cook blueberries from scratch and make them taste good. They often need help with the concrete steps, and the marketplace has responded to that.

It's affected the way I practice. In my presentations, I try to do three things. First, I invite people to look at their highest visions of what human beings can be—an aspirational component. I'm convinced that human beings are mostly aspirational. With a little bit of help, they can figure out how to make muffins if you can get them pumped up to see why blueberries will keep them alive. Second, I'm always trying to elevate or expand people's consciousness—an awareness component. That's where my discussions with inside partners (program coordinators) starts because I get more of a baseline of what people are grappling with, what they know, and what they'd like to know. Third, I'm dealing with action steps. I do get to action strategies, techniques, tips, tools, and reinforcement, but I give them a home with the aspirational awareness before I get to action. That's been reinforced by watching so many people looking for that action-oriented recipe book.

I've also become a bigger believer in diversity. In a lot of situations in which I've been invited to speak solo, I try to bring a partner or recruit an inside partner which is even better because I can plan and build capacity with that inside person just by getting ready to do the presentation. I'm dealing with my mission-centric thinking even before the presentation. Some inside partners are squeamish about sharing what they know. So I'm actually working on fear, transforming it into partnership. I serve as the safety net as I am not going to let anyone drown, but they're participating in real time in getting stronger at being internal facilitators and internal guides.

I am convinced that the wisdom is in the collective, in the collaboration. Some of the insights will come from the backstage rehearsals of the diverse team, and the more diverse the better. Some things I may want to consider are educational background, gender, age, and life history. Learning is more powerful when you have differences within the group. Development, not perfectionism, needs to have a bigger piece of your priority pie.

TECHNIQUES FOR CONFLICT RESOLUTION

Dr. Gordon grounds his presentation in his beliefs about leadership and training. He believes that it is important to understand human dynamics, including the relationships of people in the program before identifying techniques. Once people have a sense of the bigger picture, it is possible to think about techniques and training to help people and teams manage conflict better. Training involves helping people develop the characteristics associated with more successful conflict resolution.

Coaching, facilitation, and mediation are approaches that have been studied extensively and can be used to resolve conflicts. Some institutions have invested in a particular approach to conflict resolution, so it is important for leaders to be aware of institutional commitments to particular processes.

Brubaker, Noble, Fincher, Park, and Press (2014) suggest there has been a shift in the approach to conflict resolution in work environments toward an emphasis on prevention and a shift to conflict-resolution approaches that fit an institution's culture and values.

At the Leadership Institute at Community College of Philadelphia, as alluded to in the interview with Dr. Gordon, participants sometimes encounter conflict related to the team project. Underneath the conflict are often the differences in perception and beliefs that come with the intentional creation of diverse teams. It is a good idea to anticipate the potential for conflict and provide some tools for teams to attempt to resolve differences themselves.

Shapiro (2015) advocates creating "rules" at the start of a team relationship to reduce the probability of later conflict. One approach she suggests is to start with a boilerplate with the top 10 rules for the team. Everyone on the team creates a list of their top 10 on a flip chart and participants vote for 10 rules by checking them off across the various suggestions. The items with the most votes become the team rules.

A more extensive approach to reducing the probability of conflict before it occurs is provided by Toegel and Barsoux (2016). They suggest that teams have conversations about potential differences in five topic areas:

1. Appearance: People make quick early judgments, sometimes without clear awareness, based on how people look and sound. A suggested question to start discussion on this topic is, "In your world, what makes a good/bad first impression?"
2. Actions: Beliefs about appropriate behaviors are a potential source of conflict. A sample question is, "In your world, how important are punctuality and time limits?"
3. Language: Communication styles and preferences vary. A question to discuss is, "In your world, do interruptions signal interest or rudeness?"
4. Mindset: Differences in the way people think about the work they are doing can lead to conflict. A question to prompt discussion is, "In your world what's more important—the big picture or the details?"
5. Emotions: People differ in sensitivity and how they express emotion. A question to ask is, "In your world, how would you react if you were annoyed with a teammate (with silence, body language, humor, through a third party)?"

Toegel and Barsoux acknowledge that their approach is time consuming. They assert, however, that time spent dissecting team differences in perception and perspective can help avert problems later.

Sometimes a team is unable to resolve a conflict themselves. Brett and Goldberg (2017) provide a useful guide for a leader attempting to resolve a conflict between team members. They provide advice in response to questions such as "Why rely on mediation and not your authority?" "Should you initially meet with each person separately or jointly?" "What are the pitfalls to avoid?" For example, their advice for "What should you accomplish at the first meeting?" includes explaining the leader's role as finding a mutually agreeable resolution, ensuring that there are not negative consequences for the team or institution, and having people leave the meeting feeling respected and less emotional.

There is a wealth of information on conflict resolution. A realistic goal for a conflict-resolution session is to expose people to some basic techniques and to make them aware that there are resources for resolving conflict. Participants should leave the session with an understanding that they may need to invest some time beyond the leadership program if they want to improve their conflict-resolution skills.

SUMMARY OF IDEAS

1. Conflict is inevitable but can be managed in an institution.
2. An external presenter is a good choice for a presentation on conflict resolution.
3. There are evidence-based techniques for managing conflict and some institutions have preferred approaches.
4. Participants will need to practice conflict-resolution techniques beyond the leadership program to enhance their skills.

Chapter Seven

Decision Making

LEARNING GOALS

- Understand some of the influences on decision making.
- Gain ideas for practical techniques to demonstrate decision making.

All of us make decisions every day in our personal lives and at work—some with minor and some with major implications. Just because we are experienced decision makers does not mean we are effective decision makers. Most people can recall decisions that did not lead to expected outcomes. Decisions made by leaders drive organizational strategy and institutional focus and, as a consequence, have the potential to impact most, if not all, constituents of an institution. It is no wonder that effective decision making appears on lists as an important leadership skill. Participants in a leadership program will have a specific interest in understanding if it is possible to improve the ability to make sound decisions. Thus, the literature on decision making is an important content area for designers of leadership development programs.

INFLUENCES ON DECISION MAKING

There are many factors that influence the decisions we make, and many of the factors can derail good judgment. Something as simple as the time of day is related to differences in decision making. (See textbox 7.1 for a clever example.) Another significant factor is emotion (see Lerner, Li, Valdesolo, and Kassam, 2015, for a review of the literature). Most people can understand how an incident that makes someone angry in the morning may affect an unrelated decision afterward. Likewise, most people will understand how feeling grateful for the generosity of a colleague may impact the decision to support a program. Emotions affect how we think about situations, how deeply we process information, and how we respond to events and people.

EXAMPLE OF TIME EFFECT ON DECISION MAKING

Three men held in Israeli prisons appeared before a parole board. The board granted freedom to one. Was it

1. Case 1 (heard at 8:50 a.m.) Arab Israeli, 30-month sentence for fraud
2. Case 2 (heard at 3:30 p.m.) Jewish Israeli, 16-month sentence for assault
3. Case 3 (heard at 4:25 p.m.) Jewish Israeli, 30-month sentence for fraud

The discussion that follows is always interesting but almost never centered on the time factor. (Tierney, 2011)

The pervasiveness of evidence on the impact of emotions on performance may explain why the concept of emotional intelligence, or the awareness and management of one's emotions and the emotions of others, is embraced in popular literature on leadership even while the validity of the concept and its measurement are debated. Techniques for reducing the impact of emotion on decision making include delaying the decision; reframing the situation that created the emotion; discussing options with another, more objective person; and increasing focus on the thought processes being used for a decision.

New techniques are also coming from the literature on choice architecture. If we structure the procedures we use and the environment for making decisions, it may be possible to counteract some of the impact of emotion on decision making (see Beshears and Gino, 2015, for example).

Presenters should be familiar with the literature on cognitive biases or traps in decision making. Participants like knowing about biases because they almost always can think of a time when they fell into a "trap" in thinking, and it is encouraging to know that there is an explanation for why errors happen. It is easy to find articles on this topic that participants can use, regardless of their backgrounds. In 2015, the *Harvard Business Review On-Point* magazine published an edition on *The Art of Decision Making* (Ignatius, Ed.) that includes reprints of articles that reflect classic and more contemporary research on the topic. While the information in this edition is not specific to higher education, it is easy to find examples from higher education to complement the articles.

Confirmation bias, for example, is one of the traps frequently identified. We all have a tendency to look for information that supports our current viewpoint. It seems unlikely that a person preparing a presentation for the board of trustees about increasing the number of high school students taking college classes on campus is going to search out any information that does not support that point of view. But missing that information can lead to unexpected outcomes related to the decision. Faculty, for example, may have reservations about having high school students in a class, believing it may lead them to self-censor their lectures. Or the institution may be required to pay for background checks for faculty and staff because there are underage persons on campus, skewing the budget for the initiative.

Confirmation bias can explain campus tensions related to conservative and liberal beliefs and how decisions in either direction may be interpreted as bias on the part of a decision maker. A good exercise is to have participants analyze the decisions various colleges have made about speakers on campus. These decisions and the reactions to them by different groups are good illustrations of confirmation bias.

Other biases in the literature like the status quo bias, anchoring, and framing are also easy to identify in a higher education context. (See Table 7.1 for a list of some common cognitive biases and examples.) Just knowing about biases does not guarantee that a leader will be totally free from them, but awareness is the starting point for adopting intentional strategies to minimize bias.

Beyond cognitive biases and traps are other factors that hinder decision making. Not making a decision is a decision. Participants need to understand that failure to act or spending too much time investigating or reflecting on a problem can have negative consequences, including creating an impression that a leader is ineffective. We may rely too much or not enough on others in making decisions.

And of course, the unexpected may occur. A shift in public policy, for example, may require a leader to pivot rather than continue with an earlier strategy. It is impossible to cover every contingency in a presentation on decision making but providing illustrations of some potential problems helps participants realize that they need to be aware of this literature to increase their potential to be effective decision makers.

PRESENTER VIEWPOINT

A good choice for a presenter on decision making is a senior leader at the institution. The benefits of having a campus leader as a presenter include

Table 7.1. Common Cognitive Biases

COGNITIVE BIAS	DESCRIPTION
Anchoring	The tendency for an early piece of information to influence the perception of later information.
Higher education example: Admissions staff who see the high school attended by a student will evaluate the rest of the student's qualifications based on the perception of the high school (Seltzer, 2016).	
Confirmation	The tendency to look for information that supports our current viewpoint.
Men were more likely to post negative online responses and women were more likely to post positive online responses to articles about bias against women in science, engineering, technology, and math (Moss-Racusin, Molenda, & Cramer, 2015).	
Framing	The way alternatives are presented influences the response, even when the alternatives are equivalent.
Higher education example: Students were less likely to agree to a financial contract if it was framed as a loan than if it was a financially equivalent contract but did not use the word loan (Caetano, Palacios, & Patrinos, 2011).	
Groupthink	A bias for going along with a group's thinking and decisions rather than voice dissent. Groupthink leads to extreme decisions.
Higher education example: Some colleges have experienced a resistance to having speakers whose views conflict with college norms (Flaherty, 2017, March).	
Hindsight	The tendency to think events are more predictable than they are after an outcome is known.
Higher education example: An administrator hires a direct report. After providing feedback of inadequate performance, the employee is terminated. Human Resources states the administrator should have noticed red flags in the employee's application (adapted from Roese & Vohs, 2012).	
Status Quo	A preference for keeping things as they are either by not acting or making a decision not to change.
The American Council on Education (2016) reported that the number of women on governing boards in higher education has been approximately 30% for almost two decades.	

showing support for the program, "humanizing" the leader, and providing a window into how a successful leader approaches making decisions. The campus leader can start with an overview of his or her path to the leadership position.

Personal characteristics and experiences are factors in decision making. The writer Anais Nin is often credited with suggesting that "we don't see things as they are, we see things as we are." A leader who is willing to consider how personal characteristics or experiences may influence a point of view provides a model for participants to engage in self-reflection. Favorite quotes on leadership are an alternative way to illustrate the presenter's viewpoint if the presenter does not want to delve into personal experiences.

The leader can use the presentation as an opportunity to explain how the agenda for his/her area of responsibility or the institution's agenda is reflected in the decisions made. For example, has the institution committed to student success, data-driven decision making, and/or effective use of technology? Sharing an agenda illustrates the intentionality of decision making.

Of course, having an agenda can make the leader a target. At a presentation several years ago, the speaker cautioned participants to watch out for "alligators." Most people know the characteristics of alligators. When asked, participants in the audience quickly came up with characteristics such as

1. They can seem to be visible and invisible at the same time.
2. They are strong.
3. They are very fast.
4. They can hurt you.
5. They are difficult to get away from if they catch you.

Alligators are a good visual representation for the people or situations that can derail a decision maker or institution. Discussed in that context, people can usually identify "alligators" in their professional lives: the media, people who do not want you to succeed, an email sent to the wrong person, a hot-button issue. Examples abound in higher education.

Once a leader is in the grip of an "alligator," it can be challenging to change course, but it is possible to avoid "alligators" or lessen their impact. For example, regarding media communications, many institutions require that particular staff speak for the institution. Sometimes the decision maker is not the actual target, the institution is. In either case, it is important to have a strategy for dealing with "alligators."

IMPROVING DECISION MAKING

Research suggests that decision-making ability can improve. For example, decisions can be fairer if there is a way to mask personal characteristics. The television program *The Voice* has competitors perform with the judges facing away from them. This practice forces the decision makers to concentrate on the performance instead of competitors' appearance. Similarly, some faculty grade without knowing the student author of an essay to reduce any potential bias they may have about the student based on past experiences.

There are other strategies for avoiding cognitive traps that participants can use immediately. Most people are familiar with the strategy of creating a list of pros and cons before making a decision. Unfortunately, lists of pros and cons may be subject to confirmation bias or other forms of bias, so it is helpful to introduce participants to more evidence-based alternatives.

In Deborah Rowland's 2016 article about why leadership development is not developing leaders, she argues that people need more practice making decisions. Mini practice opportunities for participants to try out techniques during the presentation can enhance participants' confidence in and understanding of the techniques. The pre-mortem technique and the ten-step method are two techniques that are easy to illustrate quickly.

Consider the following scenario: Imagine that the school district has invited organizations to apply to manage underperforming public schools. The community college is selected as one of the organizations that will manage a public high school. Three years later, the student outcomes have not improved and the operation has been a strain on the college's budget. For two minutes have participants write down as many reasons as they can think of for this failure. Then have them compare notes with another participant before the entire group shares reasons for the outcome.

The pre-mortem technique (e.g., Klein, 2007) gets people to imagine that any decision they make has failed, such as in the above scenario. The rationale of the pre-mortem technique is that people are better at identifying problems or criticisms when they know the outcome, a positive version of the hindsight bias. Research shows this technique also reduces overconfidence and reduces suppression of dissenting opinions when used with a group. And, if people can anticipate a negative outcome, they may be able to make a different decision or develop strategies to reduce the risk of failure based on the issues identified up front. One Community College of Philadelphia participant's response to the use of this technique speaks to its effectiveness:

> The technique of pre-mortem has completely changed the way I make decisions. When I [consider] possibilities of failure, the technique shows me where I can improve now so that I can ensure the success of a particular project or task.

The Ten-Step Method of Decision Making was developed by Pekel and Wallace (1998). They argue that an advantage of this approach is its focus on stakeholders, ethical principles, and systems. The technique works well when there is sufficient time to work through many or most of the steps. It incorporates an aspect of the pre-mortem technique in the form of identifying a "worst-case scenario." And while all of the steps are valuable if there is time, it is possible to engage in an abbreviated version of the 10 steps that reduces the time required while adding a logic to the decision-making process. The 10 steps are

1. Identify key facts.
2. Identify and analyze major stakeholders.
3. Identify underlying driving forces.
4. Identify and prioritize operating values and ethical principles.
5. Decide who should be involved.
6. Determine and evaluate viable alternatives.
7. Test preferred alternatives with a worst-case scenario.
8. Add a preventive component.
9. Build a short- and long-term plan.
10. Use a decision checklist.

After practicing some of the steps with a scenario, participants should see the advantage of this technique for decisions when there is the luxury of time.

Case studies are another way to give people quick practice in decision making by engaging them in thinking through challenging scenarios. Good sources of cases are those adapted from actual situations that are described in college and university publications like the *Chronicle of Higher Education* and *Inside Higher Education*. Another potential source for cases is *The Leadership Dialogues* by Tyree, Milliron, and de los Santos (2004).

An example of a situation that can be crafted into a quick case study is a situation described by Becker (2002) in which she made a controversial decision about removing a student's photography exhibit from a public corridor because of the sensitivity of the photographs. (See Table 7.2 for an example of a case presentation based on the article.)

The presenter can walk people through the case, stopping at critical judgment points for participants to make decisions about what to do, identify "traps," and discuss their ideas briefly. More information is then given, eventually revealing what happened in the actual situation, in this case, a dilemma pitting sensitivity to audiences versus free speech. Participants will be reminded of their institution's policies as they discuss cases such as handling a complaint from a student about sexual harassment by a faculty member, finding that a colleague is engaged in fraudulent activity, or deciding when information is confidential versus the need for transparency.

CLOSING THE SESSION

A useful way to end the session is to circle back to any goals that were provided at the start to find out if people believe all of them were met. The presenter may also close with some quotes or advice from valued leadership books or from a book the group was assigned to read. For example, a piece of advice that hits home with participants comes from Perry Smith's *Rules and Tools for Leaders*. He suggests before making an important decision, consid-

Table 7.2. Case Example: Trial by Fire

PowerPoint Slide #1	The college tradition is for the top photography student to hang a series of photographs with a theme in the public hallway of the main campus building. The selected student hangs her work. It is an exhibit highlighting degradation of women. The graphic exhibit includes close-ups of body parts, some mutilated.
PowerPoint Slide #2	The day after the exhibit goes up, you, the acting dean, get an alarmed call. The college is scheduled to have 200 children, ages 7 to 13, on campus. They have to walk through the public hallway to get to the cafeteria. What are the issues? What do you do?
PowerPoint Slide #3	Imagine you call the department head and ask if he can get the student to move the exhibit from the public corridor to the photography department around the corner. The student agrees but writes on the wall in the public corridor that she has been censored and forced to move the exhibit. She names you as the person responsible. What are the issues? What do you do? What do you predict happens next?
PowerPoint Slide #4	Consequences of the Actual Case Wanted posters and graffiti calling the acting dean a fascist. Articles in local papers and discussion on radio programs. Debate among faculty, causing schisms.

ering the CNN rule: How will I feel if my family, friends, and neighbors hear about this decision on CNN?

SUMMARY OF IDEAS

1. There are multiple factors that influence decision making, including emotions and biases.
2. Awareness of cognitive traps and biases in decision making is the first step in minimizing them.
3. A senior college leader is a good choice for a presentation on decision making.
4. Giving participants opportunities to practice decision-making techniques during the session enhances their understanding and increases their confidence.

Chapter Eight

Diversity and Inclusion

LEARNING GOALS

- Understand the importance of including diversity and inclusion as a session topic.
- Gain ideas from one expert's approach.
- Acquire insights on designing a plan for a session on diversity and inclusion.

Many institutions of higher education have a goal, objective, or core value related to diversity. In recent years, institutions have added inclusion as a distinct but related concept. The emphasis on diversity and inclusion is also reflected in the agendas of national organizations like the American Association of Community Colleges and the Association of American Colleges and Universities. Organizations such as these are advocates for the idea that diversity and inclusion are important aspects of an institutional focus on equity and social justice.

Definitions for diversity and inclusion vary. For example, some institutions include differences in thinking style or approach as part of the definition for diversity, while others do not. Some institutions limit their approach to diversity to the United States, while others have a global focus. For purposes of clarity, in this chapter, definitions by Ferdman (2014) are used. Diversity refers to "the representation of multiple identity groups and their cultures in a particular organization or work group" (p. 3). Inclusion refers to "how well organizations and their members fully connect with, engage, and utilize people across all types of differences" (p. 4).

Sherbin and Rashid (2017) argue that diversity without inclusion does not work. Diversity can occur merely with numerical representation. Representation, however, does not capture the quality of experience people have in an environment. Without inclusion, a perception may develop that leadership is merely interested in meeting a numerical goal. This perception can foster resentment both on the part of the traditionally underrepresented and the majority. Sherbin and Rashid identify four factors associated with inclusive environments:

1. Inclusive leadership involves making sure people sense they are part of a team.
2. Authenticity occurs when people believe they can be their true selves in the environment.
3. Networking and visibility come from having a senior-level leader who acts as a sponsor.
4. Clear career paths provide an unambiguous explanation of what is necessary to succeed.

Program participants should consider the extent to which their institution reflects the characteristics of an inclusive organization in addition to considering how diverse the organization is.

Conversations about diversity and inclusion are timely and essential. Rudgers and Peterson (2017) warned that colleges and universities must be prepared for "collisions over campus climate." In the wake of the 2016 presidential election, they identified numerous issues related to diversity and inclusion that they expected to be the source of campus tensions. Although not new issues, they include

- the climate for women and people of color,
- hate speech,
- uncertainty about immigration policies,
- enforcement of Title IX,
- activism around allegations of sexual misconduct, and
- responses to the symbolism of a racial past, that is, controversy over campus statues and names of facilities.

They also identified differences over free speech and the climate for the diversity of ideas as noteworthy trends in higher education. How should college leaders respond when students object to speakers with particular points of view? How should leaders respond when students object to faculty comments that are perceived as evidence of bias? How should leaders respond to activism on and off of college campuses? What happens if faculty members are verbally attacked because of their views?

The Society for College and University Planning, in their spring 2017 report on trends in higher education, likewise identified "campus culture in flux" as a major social trend. They posed a question appropriate for college leaders: "What steps could you take to create the right environment for open discussion of difficult issues?" Leaders must understand and be prepared for a volatile issue that exists or may erupt at a college. Since social media makes communication immediate, leaders do not necessarily have time for reflection before they need to act.

Proactive leadership for Rudgers and Peterson involves institutional self-evaluation, anticipating challenges, and confronting them. Leaders must decide how to express and implement a commitment to diversity and inclusion. That means that leaders need a point of view that has been developed thoughtfully over time and that remains open to the ideas of others. A leadership program is an excellent forum for asking people interested in leadership to think about their beliefs and experiences with diversity and inclusion as well as to think about the policies and practices of their institution.

Diversity has been a session topic of the Leadership Institute at Community College of Philadelphia since the beginning. The topic aligns with the college's statement that diversity is a core institutional value. Over time, inclusion, equity, and social justice have become part of the institutional conversation about diversity, adding further context for the relevance of the topic for the Leadership Institute. Having diversity as a core value does not mean, however, that participants start out enthusiastic about the topic. Past experiences with discussions of diversity make some people apprehensive about engaging in diversity conversations. The program coordinators must anticipate the potential for apprehension and design the session to provide the right climate for reflection, consistent with the goals of the program.

The program coordinators for Community College of Philadelphia's Leadership Institute engaged a consultant, Dr. Ana Maria García, to facilitate the session on diversity and inclusion. Dr. García is an associate professor and chair of the Department of Sociology, Anthropology and Criminal Justice at Arcadia University. She is an experienced diversity trainer and presenter. The decision to use an external presenter was primarily based on a knowledge of Dr. García's work, her experience in academic and work settings, and the convenience of location.

Dr. García's presentation has been well received by participants in the Leadership Institute in part because her approach coincides with the institutional perspective and resonates with participants. She believes "the work of diversity is the work of social justice." Her model for diversity and change, adapted from Bunch (1979), includes four components:

1. Description: People must learn to articulate their perceived reality. In order to change one's own perspective or the perspective of others, we have to first describe how we see things.
2. Analysis: A logical step beyond describing how we perceive things is to ask why the situation we perceive exists. Does someone or some group benefit?
3. Vision: Vision involves an intentional choice to imagine what should exist.
4. Strategy: Strategy is the how. If we envision a change, what are the decisions and steps necessary to make change happen?

Dr. García's presentation combines an opportunity for perspective taking and future goal setting. Both of these activities have been found to be effective approaches to diversity training.

An example of perspective taking and its effects comes from Lindsey, King, Membere, and Cheung (2017) who asked research participants to assume the perspective of someone different from themselves. They asked the participants to write about the challenges faced by LGBTQ persons or racial/ethnic minorities. The researchers report that this perspective-taking exercise resulted in more positive attitudes toward others and that the effect was long lasting. Further, they report that having people set measurable but attainable goals for diversity is associated with more positive attitudes toward diversity later.

Findings such as these may explain the overwhelmingly positive responses to Dr. García's presentation. Participant comments include

- We all carry our own unconscious projections on every issue.
- Self-reflection, vulnerability, social organizing, social strategies, and a political mind are needed to address or promote change.
- I wish we could have more conversations about this topic.
- She helped me think about the various isms that keep people down.
- I feel like I am more aware of how I am seen by others in terms of culture, race, etc., as well as how I view others.

Such responses confirm that an effective presenter makes it possible for participants to have a meaningful conversation with an emphasis on the implications for leadership.

STEPS FOR CREATING A DIVERSITY AND INCLUSION PRESENTATION

Step 1: Decide where to place the session on diversity and inclusion within the context of the overall program. This decision is part of the early programming decisions. The diversity session at Community College of Philadelphia was intentionally placed later in the year and after the session on conflict resolution. By that time, participants had multiple experiences working with each other and as members of a team. We attribute the success of the session in part to the decision to have the session at a point when participants would be comfortable being more open in the conversation.

Step 2: Decide on the goal for the session. Unless there are multiple sessions on the topic of diversity and inclusion, it is best to have a tightly focused goal consistent with the amount of time available. It is important to make sure that there is an emphasis on the role of the leader in an institution's commitment to diversity and inclusion as well as the role of the leader as a change agent. Ferdman (2014) identified the following behaviors as examples of inclusive leadership:

- Hold oneself and others accountable for creating an inclusive culture.
- Invite engagement and dialogue.
- Model bringing one's whole self to work and give permission for and encourage others to do so.
- Foster transparent decision making.
- Understand and engage with resistance.

To understand and talk about how inclusion connects to the mission and vision, Gallegos (2014) suggests that "rather than relying on finding quick solutions, leadership is more productively focused on asking the right questions and acknowledging that diversity and inclusion are systemic challenges with no ready answers."

Step 3: Identify a presenter. Once the coordinators of the program are clear about the intention of the session, it is possible to identify an appropriate presenter. The presenter's skill set must include content knowledge in addition to experience with facilitation. The presenter may be a member of the college community or an external person with relevant experience. A skilled presenter will work with the program coordinators to design a session that aligns with the program and session goals. Any issues that have surfaced at this point in the program are shared with the presenter for a more targeted session focused on participant needs.

Step 4: Identify resources for the session. Review potential resources with the presenter beforehand. The readings and other materials for the session will signal the direction for the conversation. If the institution has a diversity plan, it should be included in the materials and shared with the presenter ahead of time. If the institution has statements or materials related to diversity and inclusion, they should also be included.

Other resources that may be present at the institution include scorecards for progress on diversity issues, rubrics for cultural competence, or a checklist for equity mindedness. Knowing what resources already exist helps identify the starting point for the conversation. If diversity resources such as these are not currently available at the institution, it may be possible to develop materials in conjunction with the presenter or to have a discussion about why the information does not exist. Case studies are also a viable option for prompting a leadership conversation. There are many examples of leader decisions related to diversity issues that can be demonstrated through a case study. (See Table 8.1 for an example.)

If the session is short, part of the design of the program may include prework by the participants. One possible assignment is to consider taking a test of implicit bias. Project Implicit (https://implicit.harvard.edu/implicit/) is a collaboration of researchers studying hidden biases. The test is free and voluntary. Without revealing individual results, program participants can get a sense of the extent to which they may have biases related to various groups and as a group can discuss the idea of bias and how that knowledge may influence leadership.

A less personal approach may involve reviewing campus diversity data before the session and coming prepared to discuss any differences. The Center for Urban Education (CUE) has developed the concept of "equity-mindedness." Equity-mindedness involves understanding that racial and ethnic differences may be based on institution policies, structures, and practices, not ability.

CUE created equity-minded tools to help institutions make changes to address inequity. Tools include an equity-minded checklist to help colleges and universities think about their data. The checklist can be modified to include items important for 2-year institutions. Another tool developed by CUE is the Equity Scorecard, "a theory-based strategy that assists community colleges in embedding equity into their institutional norms, practices, and policies." Felix, Bensimon, Hanson, Gray, and Klingsmith (2015) highlight its use with a specific community college.

Reading about the approach to diversity and inclusion in nonacademic environments may spark ideas for participants. Many employers are advocates for diversity and inclusion in the workplace. Employer commitment to diversity and inclusion is based in large part on logic and data showing the benefits of a diverse workforce. Johnson (2017) interviewed CEOs about their commitment to diversity. The CEOs identified four lessons for leaders:

1. Lead by example.

Diversity and Inclusion 67

Table 8.1. Case Example: Diversity Training Debate

PowerPoint Slide #1	A female faculty member (Faculty A) participates in a diversity training at another institution. She describes the experience as "transformative." After discussing the training with a few of her colleagues, she approaches the dean about having the same training at your institution on a weekend on a voluntary basis. She states that she is willing to promote the event. Are there any leadership issues?
PowerPoint Slide #2	After getting approval for the training, the faculty member sends an email blast to everyone in the division touting the benefits of the program and encouraging people to sign up to attend. A male colleague (Faculty B) responds that such training is an anti-intellectual waste of time. He objects to being asked to attend. Are there any leadership issues?
PowerPoint Slide #3	Several faculty members respond stating that they are eager to attend the session and suggesting that the objecting faculty member is racist. The dean writes that she agrees that the training would be beneficial. She adds that it is "inappropriate and unprofessional to make disparaging comments to undermine colleagues with whom we disagree." Are there any leadership issues?
PowerPoint Slide #4	A faculty member in another division then writes that the faculty member who objected was just saying in public what many faculty were saying in private—they do not want to devote more time to what he describes as the seemingly endless number of administratively driven surveys and trainings that take time away from faculty work. Are there any leadership issues?
PowerPoint Slide #5	The dean sends a letter to Faculty B asking to meet with him to discuss her expectations for professional behavior. When Faculty B refuses to meet to discuss that topic, the dean refuses to support any travel or research until he agrees to meet with her. In addition, Faculty A files a formal complaint stating that Faculty B has been engaged in strident unprofessional exchanges with her over the course of a year. Are there any leadership issues?

2. Hold yourself and others accountable.
3. Foster diversity at every level of the organization.
4. Constantly work to broaden your own perspective.

Case studies from different companies can be useful for discussing related college diversity and inclusion initiatives. For example, Deloitte made a decision to eliminate employee affinity groups defined by demographic differences and replace them with inclusion councils. Yelp is using data to track the effectiveness of diversity and inclusion initiatives. Leadership program participants can discuss the implications for higher education. Should the college embrace one of the approaches used by business? How do we prepare students to work in environments with different approaches to diversity and inclusion?

Step 5: Develop the plan for the session. This may be managed by the presenter but the coordinators need to know the session plan. Ground rules are important for challenging conversations. Thompson (2017) used mindfulness practices to successfully guide a session on diversity. She included

- Approach the conversation with openness.
- Stay engaged versus shutting down.
- Use coping strategies like deep breathing.
- Avoid judgment.
- Accept the perceptions of others as their perceptions.
- Be supportive of others.

Research suggests mindfulness may decrease implicit bias and help people regulate emotions.

Step 6: Prepare an assessment tool. It is valuable to get feedback after each session. The feedback tool should be the same as is used for other sessions.

SUMMARY OF IDEAS

1. Diversity and inclusion are timely topics for a leadership program.
2. It is important to be transparent concerning the definitions of diversity and inclusion.
3. Thinking carefully about the timing of the presentation as well as the goal for the presentation are important first steps.
4. A well-designed plan utilizing a credible presenter and multiple resources leads to an effective session.

Part III

Evaluation and Sustainability

Chapter Nine

Is It Working?

LEARNING GOAL

- Consider various short-term and long-term approaches to assessing leadership program impact.

Accounting for a leadership program's success is an inherent part of its positive evolution and sustainability. Program assessment takes its direction from the purpose and goals of the program. Assessment begins with a pre/post self-assessment tool that asks participants to rate themselves along a continuum as to their competence and knowledge in the areas outlined in the program goals. Evaluations after each session, at the midpoint, and at the end of the program provide a wealth of information about what participants are gaining and what still needs attention.

Follow-up interviews upon completion of the program provide a more personalized approach to assessing the impact of the program goals and their application in an individual's professional development plans. Follow-up with program alumni a year after the program adds to a longer-term understanding of overall effectiveness. Keeping track of promotions of program alumni provides a more quantitative rendering of the aim of developing leaders to take greater positions of responsibility in various areas of higher education.

PRE/POST ASSESSMENT

Pre/post assessment of the leadership program is a helpful tool for measuring the value added as it relates to overall program goals. It is useful to both coordinators and participants in enabling them to see the gains made as well as to determine areas that need further attention. (See Appendix S for a sample pre/post self-assessment tool.) This tool was designed using the program goals established by Community College of Philadelphia's Leadership Institute and outlined in Chapter 2.

For a more informal pre/post assessment, application responses as to motivation for applying to the leadership program are collected. Responses are anonymously shared with the cohort as part of community building and understanding of mutual goals at the first meeting, and they are also used as an informal assessment at the end of the program. One way to do this is to tape each participant's initial statement of motivation to his/her name tent at the last session and have each person provide an oral response as to the fulfillment of those motivational goals.

Colleges may also decide to use the American Association of Community College's competencies for leadership in community colleges as its overall goals and thus design a pre/post assessment based on the competencies. This framework is useful in measuring individual leadership development progress as well as the direction of institutional progress in preparing present and future leaders. (See https://www.aacc.nche.edu/wp-content/uploads/2017/09/AACC_Core_Competencies_web.pdf for a list of competencies.)

SESSION FEEDBACK

It is recommended that leadership programs offer a vehicle for feedback after each session. The information obtained provides coordinators with an understanding of session impact and areas for follow up, which can then be incorporated into group discussions at subsequent sessions. (See Appendix T for a sample session feedback form.) A summary of the session feedback is also given to presenters for their use in preparing future presentations.

At the end of the program, participants are asked to rate all sessions. This provides program coordinators with comparative information as to which sessions were most effective and which they may consider changing or eliminating in the future. (See Appendix U for a summary of sessions form.)

MIDPOINT AND FINAL EVALUATIONS

Midpoint evaluations provide a touchstone for participants in assessing their individual progress as well as their progress in relation to others in the cohort. Understandably, they only address the first half of the program goals, but reviewing their progress to this point reinforces the importance of the overall program goals and sets up an expectation of practice in assessing personal growth. (See Appendix V for a sample midpoint evaluation.)

This summative look at the midpoint provides a time to reflect on areas including what participants have learned thus far, what they see as their strengths, and how the program could provide greater benefit. Some examples of responses from Community College of Philadelphia participants include

- The single most important lesson about leadership that I have learned from the Leadership Institute is being accountable as well as adaptable toward our staff, faculty, and students here in the Athletic Center. Being a leader is a task in itself. I have learned to delegate more and communicate better by listening to the concerns and needs of our constituents.
- I believe that my organizational and analytical skills, as well as my honesty and fairness, contribute to my strengths as a leader. The Leadership Institute has helped me be more reflective in general about my leadership approach. That in itself is a good thing, and it has also led me to develop new ways of collaborating more effectively with members of my team.
- As far as developing new strengths, I'm working on trying to improve my listening skills and going along with team members' ideas, which may be very different (and sometimes better) than my own.
- Seeing leadership as risk taking is a valuable new way in which to view leadership, and one that I hadn't considered previously. In order to be a truly effective leader, it is important to take risks and recognize the real possibility of failure.
- I have learned that leadership is not just about stepping up to take the lead literally, but that it includes understanding leadership techniques that can be implemented from any station within an organization
- I think more time could be dedicated to working in groups during our sessions so we can reflect as a whole on our experiences. At times, our busy schedule makes some of the presentations feel rushed.

Final evaluations provide a culmination of participant reflections. While parts of the evaluation will naturally focus on topics covered in the second half of the program, the overall tenor of the evaluation concerns participants' growth as leaders; changes they have made or expect to make; insights gained from other leaders, including team members; and any applications made in their current positions.

Participants are also asked to comment on any changes they would make for future program cohorts and how as alumni they might contribute to the leadership program and/or other leadership efforts at the college. (See Appendix W for a sample final evaluation.) Some examples of responses from Community College of Philadelphia participants include

- When I began the Leadership Institute, I was the Coordinator of Alumni Relations and Annual Giving. Today I am the Director of Annual and Corporate Giving, and I earned an MBA degree.
- My participation in the Institute has strengthened my confidence in my ability to speak on college-related issues at the cabinet level. I feel valued as an overall contributor to the institution.
- As a result of my experience in the Leadership Institute, I began to understand the need to move away from focusing primarily on day-to-day issues and began to think more strategically and long term.
- I think about my decisions on a deeper level. When making decisions, I think about the impacts on process and on people.
- I've learned that you must make sure that what you are communicating is what is actually being received by the listener.
- An insight gained is to not be afraid of failure or success. . . . Be an irritant that encourages change.
- My approach to my work and to working with others in my area has shifted. I am concerned less with being "liked" (just being agreeable and not rocking the boat) and more with being respected as a hard worker with good ideas.
- I feel more comfortable with conflict resolution—employing better listening skills and trying to understand why it happens—the mutual needs and wants, instead of who is involved.
- Since participating in the Leadership Institute, I have had the opportunity to use the skills and knowledge gained by serving on various committees, leading roundtable discussions, advising current Institute participants, and, most importantly, leading and managing staff members with a greater understanding of college policies and networks.
- For future cohorts of the Leadership Institute, I would offer opportunities for participants to consider and identify their own professional goals within and beyond their current positions and create peer-to-peer career advising models. Because of the confidential nature of the group, participants could speak freely about desires to grow and gain understanding and advice on how to best do so.

FOLLOW-UP INTERVIEWS AND LONGER-TERM ASSESSMENT

Individual interviews scheduled a few weeks after the conclusion of the leadership program offer a more personalized approach to assessing participant growth as leaders. These interviews conducted with program coordinators also provide an opportunity for participants to discuss their intended direction in making an impact in their departments and in their professional careers. Responses on the final evaluations serve as triggers for these discussions. It is recommended that coordinators reach out to program graduates a year later (or earlier) to check on their progress and to provide feedback as needed.

Follow-up conversations with participants and their supervisors are recommended to highlight the skills and knowledge gained by their employees. With this understanding, supervisors may consider options for increased opportunities for employees to use their leadership skills for the benefit of the department.

Since a major goal of the leadership program is to develop leaders to rise to new challenges in an era of rapid change, maintaining data on graduates who were promoted to new positions or took positions with greater responsibilities serves as a visible measure of that goal. While the experience of the leadership program cannot be said to have a causal effect on promotions, it is certainly a factor in the movement of graduates on the leadership ladder.

LESSONS FROM COMMUNITY COLLEGE OF PHILADELPHIA

Outcomes for Community College of Philadelphia's Leadership Institute have exceeded expectations and have created a ripple effect at the institution. Participants overwhelmingly report greater confidence in themselves to take leadership positions, and indeed 61% of the first two cohorts, 48% of the first seven cohorts, and 35% of the first twelve cohorts have been promoted to positions of greater responsibility, either at the college or at neighboring institutions.

Team projects have directed attention, energy, and action toward improving student success, and the college has created a network of individuals who increasingly take on leadership roles in various capacities. For example, participants have eagerly accepted requests to serve on committees and college-wide initiatives; to lead cross-unit discussion groups; and to take on greater responsibilities in their departments, in professional organizations, and in their communities outside the institution. As one participant said, "I know now I can be a leader." Another participant commented: "The Leadership Institute was one of the things that inspired me to be a leader in my community and the city. At CCP, I am pushing the envelope to build a Latino agenda, something that will support and increase the Latino population at the college."

It is gratifying to observe the leadership roles our graduates increasingly take within the institution and elsewhere. Building a core of leaders open to different perspectives and willing to take on challenges stands as a promise for a stronger institution that lives its mission in ideas and action.

Chapter 9
SUMMARY OF IDEAS

1. Tie assessment directly to the program purpose and goals.
2. Utilize consistent assessments at various times during the program and at its completion to measure progress and make improvements.
3. Maintain data on program graduates to understand short-term and long-term results of program goals.

Chapter Ten

Beyond the Leadership Program

LEARNING GOAL

- Consider ideas for utilizing and strengthening skills of leadership program graduates.

Clearly, leadership development must continue beyond any one program. A conscious and deliberate effort must be made to ensure that program alumni have opportunities to hone their skills beyond what they might do on their own. At Community College of Philadelphia, we invite alumni to participate with the current class in the fall session featuring the presenter identified to discuss national issues for community colleges. This keeps graduates current on leadership issues and in touch with the program. In turn, it provides the presenter with a broader audience for interactions and feedback.

We also created a special session for alumni in the spring to involve them in ongoing conversations with leaders in the Philadelphia area. For example, alumni had a chance to learn from the CEO of a major foundation about what that organization considers when approached by an institution for support of an initiative. This topic provided new insights for alumni. Alumni are surveyed to determine topic interest and opportunities for professional growth. (See textbox 10.1 for a sample of alumni session topics.)

SAMPLE TOPICS FOR LEADERSHIP PROGRAM ALUMNI LUNCHEONS

Highs and lows of leadership, including risk taking, politics, planning, and decision making

Balancing personal and professional lives, making changes in large organizations, and risk taking for leaders

Designing high-impact goals, developing the resolve and steps to achieve them, and establishing a means to track and reinforce their progress

Leading in challenging times

Leading with purpose

The scatterbrain makings of leadership: curiosity, trust, and balance

Keeping a database of alumni enables communication, tracking of career goal progress, and supportive follow-up. Program coordinators along with senior leadership at the college may assist in matching alumni aspirations with concrete steps, including pursuing additional degrees or applying for a different position. Periodic meetings with alumni to review their career goals and the steps taken to date in reaching them help to keep them on target.

The database also serves as a resource for tapping alumni for leadership positions on committees, new initiatives at the college, and opportunities to share expertise with current program participants. Alumni may serve as recruiters for new program participants and as mentors for current project teams. Alumni are often good choices as future leadership program coordinators. They provide overall stability to the structure of the program and at the same time bring new ideas to keep the program fresh.

Some alumni may decide that they want to pursue independent study of leadership. For example, a reading/study group could be formed to sustain the momentum of the program experience and to keep the ideas churning. Other alumni turn to initiating new projects to support the college mission. A group of alumni at Community College of Philadelphia started a lunchtime "scholars" program for students interested in health careers. The purpose of the program was to improve student retention rates by focusing on affective skills—values, motivation, and attitude—regarding education and learning. Another alumni group proposed a Pathway Lecture Series to bring business leaders, scholars, and public officials to campus for discussion and debate on topics shaping public policies that impact the residents of Philadelphia.

Yet another initiative was the Executive Leadership Institute which was designed to provide Leadership Institute alumni the opportunity to reconnect with Institute colleagues on an ongoing basis, resume research activities and classroom-style discussions on leadership issues, and resume group project work in service to the college. (See Appendix X for the Proposal for Executive Leadership Institute.)

Feedback from program graduates at the conclusion of the program offers other ideas for engaging alumni. For example, one Institute alumnus suggested "Idea Parties," monthly coffee gatherings to continue to exchange ideas and support for ongoing improvements—personal and professional. Others suggested utilizing their leadership skills in the external community such as engaging in action programs involving clean up, feeding/cooking for the homeless and volunteering in city organizations. Another idea was to develop resources for archiving team project summaries to share those initiatives with a larger audience who may benefit from the results. Access to project information would also spark new ideas within the greater college community.

A frequent response from alumni was the intention to make use of the Institute network both for work and personal reasons moving forward. One alumnus stated that "the chance to connect across the departments was one of the highlights of the Leadership Institute." For example, utilizing the connections made in the Institute to better serve the college, a faculty member made plans to collaborate with a person in Student Life to implement a school spirit day. An alumna in Human Resources looked forward to planning future alternative spring breaks with teammates and the service-learning club students.

Going beyond one's institution is another possibility for further leadership development. Area community colleges with leadership programs may consider a collaborative post-leadership program initiative for alumni from their respective programs. The focus may be on executive leadership, community leadership, or a specific in-depth study of a leadership topic such as legal issues or the ethics of leadership. A survey based on institutional needs may be administered to program alumni to assess interest and solicit ideas for topics of study.

SUMMARY OF IDEAS

1. It is important to be intentional in providing further opportunities for professional growth beyond the leadership program.
2. Keeping a database of alumni enables communication for follow-up and support and serves as a resource for identifying alumni for leadership opportunities.

3. Alumni themselves are excellent sources for developing and pursuing initiatives that provide further opportunities to utilize their leadership skills.
4. Collaboration with area community colleges that have leadership programs is a way to offer program alumni opportunity for further growth in a broader context.

Concluding Thoughts and Overall Summary

Leadership development taps into the potential of people for taking the initiative and making the commitment to work within the broader context of an organization to effect change for the maximum benefit of those served. It fosters the ability of individuals to face challenges in times of crisis as well as stability.

Leadership programs are prestigious professional development initiatives, and the opportunity to interact with local and national leaders reinforces the powerful broadening experience that engenders increased confidence in skills including communication, problem solving, and decision making. All are important skills that future leaders will need in addressing the mission of community colleges with their diverse needs. When providing the right environment to learn about and exercise leadership skills and demonstrating genuine belief that the leader inside can emerge, people do rise to expectations.

We hope that readers of this book will find the experiences, guidelines, and recommendations offered helpful in building their own leadership programs and/or strengthening programs already in place. We look forward to hearing from you concerning any questions or suggestions you may have, and we stand ready to celebrate your own successes.

SUMMARY OF KEY COMPONENTS FOR A SUCCESSFUL LEADERSHIP PROGRAM

1. The program is a priority of the institution's president.
2. The program is organized with clear goals and expectations.
3. Criteria for participation is selective.

4. There is a commitment of financial assistance.
5. An effective coordinator(s) is/are in place.
6. Projects of benefit to the institution are an integral part of the program.
7. Presenters on key topics are both internal and external to the institution and have expert credentials.
8. Assessment is consistent and ongoing.
9. Sustainable contacts with alumni are planned.

Appendix A

Sample Acceptance Letter

Date
Name
Address
Philadelphia, PA

Dear Name,

It is a distinct pleasure to inform you of your selection for the eleventh annual Leadership Institute at Community College of Philadelphia. As a participant in this year's Leadership Institute, you and a diverse group of college colleagues will spend the academic year interacting with leaders in various fields related to the community college mission. You will have multiple opportunities to learn more about the internal and external environments within which the college operates, to reflect on the nature of leadership, and to put leadership skills into practice by completing a project of benefit to the college community. I know this will be an exciting year!

In July, you will be receiving a packet with more information about the Institute, including a schedule of sessions. You will also be receiving some reading materials to provide the participants with a useful starting point for reflection and sharing ideas about leadership. Finally, you will be required to complete the Herrmann Brain Dominance Instrument® Assessment which assesses thinking preferences. Information about the process for completing this assessment will be sent to you shortly.

Please confirm that you accept this opportunity to participate in the Leadership Institute by contacting (Name) in my office by e-mail at @ccp.edu or by phone at 215-751-8000 no later than July 11, 2013. I also ask that you review the dates listed in the application to confirm your commitment to attend all scheduled sessions. I look forward to seeing you at the first session on Thursday, August 29th.

Again, I congratulate you on your selection for this exciting venture.

Cordially,

Name
Vice President for Academic Affairs

Community College of Philadelphia Leadership Institute

Appendix B

Sample Rejection Letter

Date
Name
Address
Philadelphia, PA

Dear Name,

Thank you for your interest in the Leadership Institute at the Community College of Philadelphia. I regret to inform you that I am unable to extend an invitation to you for the 2009–2010 class. If you would like to discuss how you might strengthen your application for a future class, please feel free to contact (Name). I do appreciate your interest and hope you will consider applying again in the future.

Sincerely,

Name
Vice President for Academic Affairs

Community College of Philadelphia Leadership Institute

Appendix C

Sample Application

Leadership Institute 2013–2014
Community College of Philadelphia
Application

The Office of Academic Affairs is seeking applications for the eleventh annual Leadership Institute of the Community College of Philadelphia to take place during the 2013–2014 academic year.

Purpose: The major goal of the Institute is to develop leaders and potential leaders within the college community by fostering the ability of individuals to meet new challenges faced by the college in fulfilling its mission and values around access and success. The Leadership Institute provides participants with an understanding of the broader issues as well as specific strategies that will build leadership capacity in various areas of the college.

Benefits of Participation: The Leadership Institute will incorporate a variety of speakers, topics, and activities designed to enhance leadership ability by providing participants with the following opportunities:

- to interact with and gain insight from leaders in various fields related to the mission of the community college
- to increase awareness of the local, state, and national contexts within which the college functions
- to increase understanding of specific ways in which the larger environment may impact the college in the pursuit of its mission

- to develop increased self-awareness as leaders, enhance communication skills, and learn strategies for conflict resolution
- to heighten awareness of organizational structure and organizational culture
- to increase knowledge of resource allocation, budgeting, and finance
- to explore decision making in the context of individual and institutional values
- to become part of a diverse, collaborative network of problem solvers
- to work collaboratively on a project of interest to the participant and of benefit to the college community
- to gain a deeper understanding of the college mission, vision, and values

Who is eligible: The Leadership Institute invites applications from full-time faculty, administrators, and classified/confidential staff who are interested in seeking leadership positions in the future or honing their leadership skills for the positions they currently hold. Part-time faculty, administrators, and classified/confidential staff who have been continuously employed at the college for a minimum of 2 years are also welcome to apply.

Schedule: Sessions will take place during fall 2013 and spring 2014 Professional Development weeks and once a month during the fall and spring semesters **on Friday afternoons from 12:15 to 4:30 p.m.** Certificates of completion will be awarded at the College Honors Tea in spring 2014.

How to apply: An application with detailed instructions for completion is attached. The deadline for submitting applications to the Office of Academic Affairs is **5:00 p.m. on Wednesday, May 15, 2013.** No applications will be accepted after this deadline.

1. Personal Data: Please provide the information requested below.

```
Name: _____
Job Title & Rank: _____
Department: _____
Part-Time or Full-Time: _____
Work Telephone: _____
Home Telephone: _____
Email Address: _____
```

2. Professional and/or Volunteer Activities: For this section, please submit an updated CV or résumé. Be sure to proofread carefully and include the following information:

- Any college professional activities or committee involvement in which you have participated. Please describe the nature of your participation, including any leadership positions you have held.
- Any community, civic, business, or professional activities in which you have participated outside the college. Please indicate the nature of your participation, including any leadership positions you have held.

3. Letter of Application: Write a letter (not to exceed 2 double-spaced typed pages) in which you address the questions below. Be sure to respond to all parts of the questions.

- Who is the leader you admire most? What leadership qualities does this person possess? What makes him or her admirable?
- Describe a situation in your professional life in which you played a leadership role. In what ways were you effective? In what ways were you ineffective? What did you learn from this?
- Why are you interested in participating in the Leadership Institute?
- What do you believe you can contribute to the Leadership Institute?

4. References: Two letters of reference, written by colleagues with knowledge of your leadership potential, are **required**. Please list names and office phone numbers for the two colleagues you have asked to write letters of reference.

Name: _____ Ext: _____

Name: _____ Ext: _____

5. Commitment: In order for the Leadership Institute to be a success, each participant must fully participate. Sessions will take place during fall 2013 and spring 2014 Professional Development weeks and once a month on Friday afternoons during the fall and spring semesters. The opening session on August 29, 2013, will take place from 8:15 a.m. to 3:30 p.m. All other sessions are scheduled from 12:15 to 4:30 p.m. The dates for next year's Leadership Institute sessions are as follows:

August 29, 2013	January 9, 2014
September 20, 2013	February 7, 2014
October 18, 2013	February 28, 2014
November 15, 2013	March 28, 2014
December 13, 2013	April 25, 2014

Appendix C

In addition to attending all scheduled sessions of the Leadership Institute, participants will be asked to complete a team project.

Please indicate your commitment to attend **each** session of the Institute and to complete the project by signing below, and indicate the approval of your supervisor or department chair by obtaining his or her signature. Please note that if you are unable to make such a commitment for the coming academic year, there will be other opportunities to participate in the future.

Applicant's signature: _____
Date: _____

Supervisor/Department Chair's signature: _____
Date: _____

6. *Deadline:* Please submit the completed application form, CV or résumé, application letter, and letters of reference to the address below no later than **Wednesday, May 15, 2013, at 5:00 p.m.** No applications will be accepted after this deadline. Incomplete applications will not be processed. All application materials should be sent to:

Name
Vice President for Academic Affairs
Office of Academic Affairs, Rm. M2-34
Community College of Philadelphia
1700 Spring Garden St., Philadelphia, PA 19130

Please direct questions regarding the Leadership Institute and/or the application process to (Name) at @ccp.edu or Ext. xxxx.

7. *Notification:* Applicants selected to participate in the 2013–2014 Leadership Institute will be notified of acceptance the week of June 17, 2013.

Thank you for applying to the Leadership Institute 2013–2014

Appendix D

Guidelines for the Selection Committee and Selection Criteria

GUIDELINES FOR THE COMMITTEE

1. The Selection Committee is charged with selecting up to 20 participants from the pool of candidates for the Leadership Institute. The final number of participants selected is not fixed but will depend on the number of qualified applicants.
2. Up to five candidates may be placed on a waiting list. The waiting list will remain active until the week prior to the first session of the Leadership Institute for a given academic year. Thereafter, if participants must drop out of the Institute, they will not be replaced.
3. No one who is applying to participate in the Leadership Institute may be a member of the Leadership Institute Selection Committee.
4. To facilitate the selection process, the members of the Selection Committee will use a point system based on the criteria outlined (see attached grid).
5. The Selection Committee does *not* meet as a group. Your individual impressions of each candidate are important.
6. Information contained in Leadership Institute application materials and the deliberations of the Selection Committee *must* be kept confidential to protect the privacy of the candidates.

Appendix D

SELECTION CRITERIA

1. Participants in the Leadership Institute must fall into one of the following employment categories: full-time or part-time faculty, full-time or part-time staff (hourly employees), or full-time or part-time administrators. Part-time applicants must have been continuously employed at the college for a minimum of 2 years.
2. To be eligible to participate in the Leadership Institute, all candidates must sign in the space provided under item 5 on the application ("Commitment") and they must obtain the signature of their immediate supervisor or department chair.
3. Participants in the Leadership Institute should be selected to be representative of the diversity of the college workforce. Faculty, staff, and administrators from diverse cultural backgrounds and who serve in various roles within the institution should be represented. These criteria are designed to help ensure that

   - Multiple perspectives are brought to bear on the issues addressed in the Institute.
   - Participants will be able to share both breadth and depth of knowledge of the college as an institution.
   - Participants have opportunities to form working relationships with colleagues outside their own areas.
   - Communication and cooperation among employees in different areas of the college will be greatly improved over time as the Leadership Institute is repeated.

4. It is a requirement for participation in the Leadership Institute that candidates demonstrate *potential* for assuming leadership roles within the college community. A Letter of Reference containing a positive assessment of the candidate's leadership potential may be considered evidence of such potential by the committee. Also, the candidate may demonstrate such potential in the Letter of Application in one or more of the following ways:

   - Articulating a philosophy of leadership by identifying a leader and clearly linking specific leadership qualities to that individual.
   - Identifying a professional situation where the candidate took a leadership role and reflecting on the effectiveness or ineffectiveness of the leadership strategies he or she employed in this situation.
   - Linking reflection or analysis of the professional situation described above with leadership qualities the candidate admires and/or the candidate's philosophy of leadership.

Appendix D 93

- Articulating the candidate's potential contribution to the Leadership Institute.

5. It is desirable that candidates for the Leadership Institute provide evidence of service in one or both of the following ways:

    - A record of service to the college community beyond minimal job requirements, especially by assuming leadership roles.
    - A record of service to the community at large, especially by assuming leadership roles.

Community College of Philadelphia Leadership Institute

Appendix E

Selection Criteria Grid

Appendix E

Applicant Name: _____

1. Employment Category   Check appropriate status
   ___ Faculty   FT ___ PT ___
   ___ Staff   FT ___ PT ___
   ___ Administrator   FT ___ PT ___

2. Commitment (see #5 on Sample Application)
   Candidate's Signature _____
   Department Chair or Immediate Supervisor's Signature _____

Please assign quality points for each item in #3-6 below based on the following scale:

Missing	Inadequate	Adequate	Exceptional
0	1	2	3

Maximum total of points possible is 39.

3. Indication of Service   Fill in points in space provided
   · to the College   _____
   · to the Community   _____
   · as leader (either college or community)   _____

4. Philosophy of Leadership
   · identifies leader   _____
   · links qualities of leadership to leader   _____

5. Self-awareness as Leader/Potential Leader
   · identifies professional situation where leadership was called for _____
   · reflects on effectiveness/ineffectiveness of leadership
     strategies in that situation
   · explains lessons learned   _____
   · links reflection on situation to philosophy of leadership (#4)   _____

6. Potential Contributions to Leadership Institute
   · articulates interest in participating in Institute   _____
   · articulates ways of contributing to Institute   _____
   · first positive reference   _____
   · second positive reference   _____

Total number of points =

Permission granted by American Association of Community Colleges to use in *Up and Running: Starting and Growing a Leadership Program at a Community College*. (Artifact was previously published in Jeandron, C. A. [2006]. *Growing your own leaders: Community colleges step up*. American Association of Community Colleges. Washington, DC: Community College Press.)

Community College of Philadelphia Leadership Institute

Appendix F

Sample Program Schedule

OPENING SESSION (AUGUST): OFF SITE

8:15 a.m.	Continental Breakfast Served
8:45–9:00 a.m.	Welcome and Remarks
	President and/or Vice President for Academic Affairs
9:00–9:45 a.m.	*Working as a Leadership Community*
	Program Co-Coordinator
10:00–12:30 p.m.	Workshop: *Identifying Your Leadership Style*
	Selected presenter
12:30–1:15 p.m.	Catered Lunch
1:15–2:30 p.m.	Workshop: *Building Effective Teams*
	Selected presenter
2:45–3:15	*Project Overview*
	Program Co-Coordinator
3:15–3:30 p.m.	Session Evaluation and Wrap Up

Reading: Eckel, P., Green, M., Hill, B., & Mallon, W. (1999). Leading change with teams. In *Taking charge of change: A primer for colleges and universities*, pp. 27–33. American Council on Education.

SESSION 2 (SEPTEMBER): LEADERSHIP AND CHANGE AT THE LOCAL LEVEL

Selected Location

12:15–1:00 p.m.	Lunch and Guidelines for Facilitating Reading Discussions
	Pictures taken for leadership program website
1:00–2:30 p.m.	*Change Agents at a Local Level*
	Chief Education Officer, Mayor's Office, Philadelphia
2:45–3:45 p.m.	Book Discussion: *Leadership on the Line* by Heifetz & Linsky
3:45–4:15 p.m.	Project Teams Assigned; Exploring Potential Topics
4:15 p.m.	Session Evaluation and Wrap Up

Readings: College Strategic Plan
Heifetz, R. A., & Linsky, M. (2002). *Leadership on the line: Staying alive through the dangers of leading*. Boston: Harvard Business School Press.

SESSION 3 (OCTOBER): HIGHER EDUCATION LEADERSHIP AT THE STATE LEVEL

Selected Location

12:15–1:00 p.m.	Lunch and Discussion of Readings
1:00–2:30 p.m.	*Community College Leadership*
	Presidents' Panel (consisting of 3 presidents)
2:45–3:30 p.m.	*Six Thinking Hats: Now We Are Green*
	Selected presenter(s)
3:30–4:15 p.m.	Project Teams Select Topics and Initiate Working Plan
4:15 p.m.	Session Evaluation and Wrap Up

Readings: Strategic Plan or Vision for State Community Colleges
Walsh, Diana Chapman. (2006). *Trustworthy leadership*. Fetzer Institute.

SESSION 4 (NOVEMBER): NATIONAL TRENDS

Selected Location

12:15–1:15 p.m.	Lunch with Leadership Institute Alumni
1:15–2:45 p.m.	*A National Voice for Emerging Issues in Accreditation and Quality Assurance*
	President, Council for Higher Education Accreditation
3:00–4:00 p.m.	Project Teams hand in summary of research
4:00 p.m.	Session Evaluation and Wrap Up

Readings: Council for Higher Education Accreditation (November 2012), *The CHEA initiative: Final report*. http://www.chea.org/

Eaton, J. S. (June 27, 2013). It's time to speak out: Accreditation, its critics and its future. *Inside Accreditation*, 9(4).

Eaton, J. S. (June 3, 2013). Accreditation and the next reauthorization of the Higher Education Act. *Inside Accreditation*, 9(3).

SESSION 5 (DECEMBER): GRANT WRITING; PROFESSIONAL PRESENTATION

Selected Location

12:15–1:00 p.m.	Lunch and Discussion with Mentors
1:00–2:00 p.m.	*Grant-Writing Panel Discussion*
	Selected presenter(s), including grant recipients
2:15–3:45 p.m.	*Public Speech for the Polished Professional*
	Selected presenter
3:45–4:15 p.m.	Draft project proposals due with preliminary budget
4:15 p.m.	Session Evaluation and Wrap Up

Readings: Grant proposal process specific to the institution

Anderson, T. (June 2013). How to give a killer presentation. *Harvard Business Review*, pp. 121–125.

Orlando, J. (November 11, 2013). Improve your PowerPoint design with one simple rule. *Faculty Focus*.

Note: Midpoint Evaluation Online: *Due January 6*

SESSION 6 (JANUARY): COLLEGE COMMUNITY FEEDBACK ON TEAM PROJECTS

Selected Location

12:15–1:30 p.m.	Lunch and Review of Midpoint Evaluation Responses Reflection
2:00–3:30 p.m.	*Presentation of Project Proposals by Teams*
	Question and Answer Session with Members of the College Community
3:30 p.m.	Session Evaluation and Presentation Feedback

SESSION 7 (FEBRUARY): COMMUNICATION AND CONFLICT RESOLUTION

Selected Location

12:15–1:00 p.m.	Lunch and Discussion
1:00–3:00 p.m.	*Leading Conflict Resolution: The Opportunity of Ouch*
	Selected presenter
3:15–4:15 p.m.	Project Team Work Session
4:15 p.m.	Session Evaluation and Wrap Up

Readings: Fisher, R., & Ury, W. (1983). *Getting to yes: Negotiating agreement without giving in*. New York: Penguin Books.
Holton, S. A. (2002). *A tree grows through the floor*. Gabriel Ames Associates.
Perlow, L., & Williams, S. (May 2003). Is silence killing your company? *Harvard Business Review*.

SESSION 8 (MARCH): DECISION MAKING IN HIGHER EDUCATION

Selected Location

12:15–1:00 p.m.	Lunch and Discussion
1:00–3:00 p.m.	*Decision Making Workshop–Watch Out for Alligators*
	Selected presenter
3:15–3:30 p.m.	Project Updates
3:30–4:15 p.m.	Project Team Work Session
4:15 p.m.	Session Evaluation and Wrap Up

Reading: Kahneman, D., Lovallo, D., & Sibony, O. (June 2011). Before you make that big decision. *Harvard Business Review*.

SESSION 9 (APRIL): THE HIGHER ED BUDGET AND INSTITUTIONAL GOALS

Selected Location

12:15–1:00 p.m.	Lunch and Discussion
1:00–3:00 p.m.	*Balancing the Budget: A Case Study* (specific to the institution)
	Vice President for Planning and Finance
3:15–4:15 p.m.	Project Progress Reports
4:15 p.m.	Session Evaluation and Wrap Up

Readings: Case Study: College Budget
Goldstein, L. (March 2005). The flexible budget. *NACUBO Business Officer*, pp. 35–41.

SESSION 10 (MAY): LEADERSHIP AND DIVERSITY

Selected Location

12:15–1:00 p.m.	Lunch and Discussion
1:00–3:00 p.m.	*Diversity: Walking the Talk*
	Selected presenter

Readings: Community College Diversity Plan
García, A. M. (1999). Multiculturalism: An "as if" phenomenon. *Qualitative Studies in Education*, 12(3), 299–310.
TED Talk: Chimamanda Ngozi Adichie: *The danger of a single story* (July 2009). http://www.ted.com/talks/chimamanda_adichie_the_danger_of_a_single_story.html

Note: Final Evaluation Online: *Due May 10*

Appendix F

PROJECT REPORT PRESENTATIONS (MAY)

Selected Location

3:00–4:00 p.m.	Final Project Reports
4:00 p.m.	Program Wrap Up

***COLLEGE HONORS TEA:** Presentation of Certificates and Awards*
Selected Location

Community College of Philadelphia Leadership Institute

Appendix G

*Community College of Philadelphia
Leadership Institute Presenters*

Identifying Your Leadership Style and Building Effective Teams

    President of Think Good Leadership

City Trends

    Former Chief of Staff to Mayor
    Executive Director, Pennsylvania Economy League
    Executive Director, Philadelphia Workforce Investment Board
    Daily News Columnist
    President & CEO, Innovation Philadelphia
    Co-Founder and President, Philadelphia Youth Network
    Chief Education Officer, City of Philadelphia
    City Managing Director
    Executive Director, Fels Institute of Government
    Executive Director of the Philadelphia Education Fund
    Superintendent of Schools

State Trends

    Presidents' Panel: various presidents of community colleges in the region

Assessment and Utilizing Institutional Data

    Director of Institutional Research, CCP

Director of Assessment and Evaluation, CCP

National Trends

President, American Association of Community Colleges
President, American Association of Colleges and Universities
Executive Director, Middle States Commission on Higher Education
Head, Division of Government and Public Affairs, American Council on Education
U.S. Deputy Assistant Secretary for Community Colleges
Project Director, Achieving the Dream: Community Colleges Count
President and CEO, Association of Community College Trustees
President, Council for Higher Education Accreditation

Budget and Finance Basics

Vice President for Business and Finance, CCP

Grant Writing

Director, Institutional Advancement, CCP
Coordinator of Grants with Panel of Grant Recipients, CCP

Public Speech

Experts from within the Communications Department

Conflict Resolution

Professor of Communication Studies, Bridgewater State College
Executive Director, Center for Alternative Dispute Resolution
President, Taylor Training and Development
Founder & Principal, TAGA Consulting

Six Thinking Hats

Co-Coordinators of Leadership Institute

Diversity and Leadership

Associate Professor and Chair, Department of Sociology, Anthropology and Criminal Justice, Arcadia University

Leadership and Gender

President, Coalition of Labor Union Women
Executive Director, Community Women's Education Project
Executive Director, Black Women's Health Project
Executive Director, Women Against Abuse
Executive Director, CHOICE
President, Women's Way

Leadership and Emotional Intelligence

Co-Chair of Teleos Leadership Institute

Decision Making in an Institutional Context

Vice President for Academic Affairs, CCP
President, CCP

Community College of Philadelphia Leadership Institute

Appendix H

Sample Reading List

One book is selected each year to stimulate thinking about leadership and serve as a resource throughout the program.

Bolman, L. G., & Deal, T. E. (2006). *The wizard and the warrior: Leading with passion and power*. San Francisco: Jossey-Bass.
DePree, M. (1989). *Leadership is an art*. New York: Doubleday.
Gladwell, M. (2008). *Outliers: The story of success*. New York: Little, Brown and Company.
Heifetz, R. A., & Linsky, M. (2002). *Leadership on the line: Staying alive through the dangers of leading*. Boston: Harvard Business School Press.
Ibarra, H. (2015). *Act like a leader, think like a leader*. Boston: Harvard Business Review Press.

FIRST HALF OF LEADERSHIP PROGRAM

Building Teams

HBR's 10 must reads on teams. (2013). Harvard Business School Publishing Corporation.
Roberson, R. (2017, July/August). Thinking differently, together. *Business Officer*. https://www.businessofficermagazine.org/features/thinking-differently-together/
Whelan, S. A. (2005). How do high performance teams function? In *Creating effective teams*. Thousand Oaks, CA: Sage Publications.

Organizational Culture: Your institution's organization chart

Fullan, M. (2004). *Leading in a culture of change: Personal action guide and workbook*. San Francisco: Jossey-Bass.

City Trends (selections specific to an institution's city)

The Chamber of Commerce for Greater Philadelphia. (2017, March). *Roadmap for growth: Top priorities*. Philadelphia, PA.
Fels Public Policy Challenge (2010, Spring/Summer). *Penn Arts & Sciences Magazine*. University of Pennsylvania School of Arts and Sciences.
Graduate! Philadelphia: The challenge to complete (2005). A joint call to action of the Pennsylvania Economy League and the Philadelphia Workforce Investment Board. (Executive Summary)
Philadelphia Workforce Investment Board. (2014). *A tale of two cities*.

State Trends

Complete college America: Essential steps for states. (2014). Washington, DC. www.completecollege.org
Pennsylvania Commission for Community Colleges Strategic Plan 2015–2010. (selection specific to your state)
Trachtenberg, S. J. (2008, June 13). What I might have told my successor. *The Chronicle of Higher Education*, pp. A37–38.

National Trends

American Association of Community Colleges (2005). *Competencies for community college leaders*. https://www.aacc.nche.edu/wp-content/uploads/2017/09/AACC_Core_Competencies_web.pdf
Bailey, T. R., Jaggars, S. S., & Jenkins, D. (2015). *Redesigning America's community colleges: A clearer path to student success*. Boston: Harvard University Press.
Brown, J. N. (2017, Summer). 10 challenges facing community colleges. *Trustee Quarterly*.
Council for Higher Education Accreditation. (2012, November). *The CHEA initiative: Final report*. http://www.chea.org/userfiles/CHEAkry224/TheCHEAInitiative_Final_Report8.pdf
Eaton, J. S. (2013, June 27). It's time to speak out: Accreditation, its critics and its future. *Inside Accreditation*, 9(4).
McClenney, K. (2009, April). Helping community college students succeed: A moral imperative. *The Chronicle of Higher Education*, 55(33), A60.
McPhail, C. J. (2011, April). *The completion agenda: A call to action*. Washington, DC: American Association of Community Colleges.
Middle States Commission on Higher Education. (2003). *Advancing student learning. Highlights and summary of student learning assessment: Options and resources*. Philadelphia, PA: MSCHE.
A national dialogue: The Secretary of Education's Commission on the Future of Higher Education. (2006). http://www.ed.gov/about/bdscomm/list/hiedfuture/index.html
Trends for higher education: Evolution of higher education. (2017, Spring). Society for College and University Planning.

Assessment

Nunley, C., Bers, T., & Manning, T. (2011, July). *Learning outcomes assessment in community colleges*. National Institute for Learning Outcomes Assessment.

Grant-Writing Basics

Grant proposal process specific to your institution
Smith, N. B., & Tremore, J. (2008). *The everything grant writing book*. Avon, MA: Adams Media Corporation.

Public Speaking

Anderson, T. (2013, June). How to give a killer presentation. *Harvard Business Review*, pp. 121–125.
Lee, K. (2017). 10 tips for speaking like a Ted Talk pro. *American Psychological Association*, 48(2), p. 64. http://www.apa.org/monitor/2017/02/tips-speaking.aspx
Orlando, J. (2013, November 11). Improve your PowerPoint design with one simple rule. *Faculty Focus*.

SECOND HALF OF LEADERSHIP PROGRAM

Budgets and Finance: Budget and finance case studies specific to your institution

Barr, M. J., & McClellan, G. S. (2011). *Budgets and financial management in higher education*. John Wiley & Sons, Inc.
Goldstein, L. (2005, March). The flexible budget. *NACUBO Business Officer*, pp. 35–41.

Communication and Conflict Resolution

Gallo, A. (2017, July 24). How people with different conflict styles can work together. *Harvard Business Review*.
Perlow, L., & Williams, S. (2003, May). Is silence killing your company? *Harvard Business Review*.
Weisbord, M. R., & Janoff, S. (2015). Surface unspoken agreements: Finding common ground where you least expect it. In *Lead more, control less: 8 advanced leadership skills that overturn convention*. Berrett-Koehler Publishers, Inc.

Decision Making in Higher Education

Beshears, J., & Gino, F. (2015, May). Leaders as decision architects. *Harvard Business Review*.
HBR's 10 must reads on making smart decisions. (2013, March). Boston: Harvard Business Review Press.

Diversity and Inclusion

Banaji, M. R., & Greenwald, A. G. (2013). *Blindspot: Hidden biases of good people*. New York: Bantam Books.
Ferdman, B. M., & Deane, B. R. (Eds.). (2014). Diversity at work: The practice of inclusion. San Francisco: Jossey-Bass.
García, A. M. (1999). Multiculturalism: An "as if" phenomenon. *Qualitative Studies in Education*, 12(3), 299–310.
Goleman, D. (2011). *Leadership: The power of emotional intelligence, selected writings*. Northampton, MA: More Than Sound LLC.
TED Talk: Chimamanda Ngozi Adichie. (2009). *The danger of a single story*. http://www.ted.com/talks/chimamanda_adichie_the_danger_of_a_single_story.html

Appendix H

OTHER SELECTIONS

Baum, D. (2000). *Lightning in a bottle: Proven lessons for leading change*. Chicago: Dearborn, a Kaplan Professional Company.
Collins, J. (2001). *Good to great*. New York: HarperCollins.
Kotter, J. P. (2012). *Leading change*. Boston: Harvard Business School Press.
Walsh, D. C. (2006). *Trustworthy leadership*. Fetzer Institute.
Watkins, J. M., Mohr, B., & Kelly, R. (2011). *Appreciative inquiry: Change at the speed of imagination*. San Francisco: John Wiley & Sons, Inc.

Community College of Philadelphia Leadership Institute

Appendix I

Checklist for Planning a Leadership Program

Application

- ☐ Post online to college community
- ☐ Hold informational workshops
- ☐ Recruit program alumni to review applications
- ☐ Request acceptance/rejection letters from senior leader overseeing program

Budget

- ☐ Calculate program finances needed and submit to senior leader overseeing program
- ☐ Expense categories to consider
    - Thinking-style inventory
    - Presenter stipends/gifts
    - Lunches
    - Books/articles
    - Trophies

Schedule

- ☐ Presenters (consider college calendar events in establishing dates)
- ☐ Reserve rooms
    - External site for opening session

- Internal rooms for cohort sessions, national presentation, and project presentations

Materials

- ☐ Thinking-style inventory
- ☐ Selected book(s) for the year
- ☐ Articles (obtain permission to reprint as needed)
- ☐ Create binders for participants to include
  - Congratulations letter from president
  - Leadership program goals
  - Cohort bios, contact information, name tents
  - Schedule for the year
  - Project guide
  - Articles (may also use electronic portfolio)
  - Organizational chart for institution and other resources
- ☐ Select assessment tool

Website

- ☐ Update leadership program bios, schedule, project summaries
- ☐ Set up discussion board

Community College of Philadelphia Leadership Institute

Appendix J

Descriptors for de Bono's Six Thinking Hats

Adapted from de Bono's *Six Thinking Hats*

Six Thinking Hats	Description	Questions to Ask
White: Information Hat	• Focus on logic, facts, and figures • Look for gaps	• What are the facts? • What information is missing? • How can we obtain additional info?
Red: Emotional Hat	• Focus on intuition, venting, hunches, instincts • Don't judge thoughts/feelings • Positive (curiosity, optimism) and negative (doubt, pessimism) feelings are ok	• How do we feel about ___? • Why do we like/dislike ___? • Why do we trust/distrust ___?
Black: Risk Hat	• Focus on critical analysis, possible problems • Be skeptical/analytical vs. pessimistic/cynical • Actively look for weak points, design flaws, risks	• Why is this not a good idea? • Why will this not work? • What are the negative consequences? • What happens if we fail?
Yellow: Benefits Hat	• Focus on positive speculation, optimism, value • Be bright, sunny, upbeat • Actively look for strong points, design benefits	• Why is this a good idea? • Why will this work? • What are the positive consequences? • What happens if we succeed?
Green: Creative Hat	• Focus on new ideas, free thinking • Anything goes: do not stifle or debate ideas • Everyone should offer at least one new idea	• What would success look like? • What has never been tried before? • What are some spontaneous ideas?
Blue: Organization Hat	• Focus on logistics, planning, next-step thinking • Typically worn by facilitator, but anyone can make procedural suggestions	• What needs to be done to implement Green Hat idea(s)? • What is our next step? • What resources do we need? • What is our time frame?

Appendix K

Four Keys to a Successful Six Thinking Hats (STH) Session

KEY #1

Always keep the discussion within the parameters of the hat currently in use. Facts are for the White Hat, emotions are for the Red Hat, planning is for the Blue Hat, etc. This allows the group to simplify its thinking by focusing on one aspect of the issue at a time.

For example, when you are inspired with a new idea, don't interrupt another hat discussion to proclaim: "I have a new idea!" Instead, make a mental or written note and wait for the Green Hat. A properly run STH session allows everyone to speak their minds within the appropriate hat.

KEY #2

Everything is fair game within the correct hat. There is no censorship of ideas or suppression of comments. The group must accept the premise that words, thoughts, and ideas are protected within the appropriate hat. If you think an idea is stupid, say so . . . during the Red Hat (or Black Hat if you can back it up with thoughtful analysis).

STH is about critiquing ideas, not the people who suggest them or the manner or timing in which they are brought up. This takes the ego out of the process. If one of your comments is picked apart by the group during the

Black Hat mode, don't take it personally—that's exactly the purpose of the Black Hat.

KEY #3

Use a moderator/facilitator. This person can act like a referee if any "rules" are being violated. This person is also very important during the Blue Hat planning mode because someone must be responsible for ensuring that ideas are put into the right context for action steps.

KEY #4

Although there is no one correct sequence to follow, try using the following order of hats.

1. Blue Hat: Facilitator/moderator provides situational overview. What's the problem and what's the group's mission?
2. White Hat: Look at the facts, figures, details. Is more information needed?
3. Red Hat: Brief venting session to deal with emotional feelings (good and bad)—helps clear the way for logical discussion.
4. Black Hat: What are the possible problems to this situation? What if we move forward and fail?
5. Yellow Hat: What are the possible benefits to this situation? What if we move forward and succeed?
6. Green Hat: New ideas: What creative solutions will address or resolve the issue?
7. Blue Hat II: What is our next step? How do we move forward? How will we monitor progress? How will we determine success or failure?
8. Red Hat II: Emotional follow-up: How does everyone feel about the group's thinking on the issue as well as the solution(s)?

Adapted from de Bono's *Six Thinking Hats*

Appendix L

Sample Project Directive

Project Goals: An essential component of the Leadership Institute is the completion of a project of benefit to the college community and of interest to you as a member of this community. A primary goal of the project is to raise awareness of institutional goals and to develop new and effective ways to work together to achieve them. A second major goal is for participants to further develop leadership abilities on an experiential level. Thus, you are encouraged to take a broad perspective on issues relevant to the projects by making use of insights gained into local, state, and national trends impacting the college and the larger community. Likewise, you are invited to draw on your increased understanding of the nature of leadership and of self in relation to others. Finally, the project will provide opportunities to draw on enhanced communication and conflict-resolution skills and develop improved strategies for navigating the complexities of our organizational culture and solving problems collaboratively.

The Theme: The theme for this year's project is "**Fostering Student Success and Making an Impact**." A major challenge facing community colleges nationwide is the fact that many of our students leave us before they have achieved their academic and personal goals. Although researchers have identified teaching strategies that correlate highly with increased student persistence and success, the responsibility for creating a welcoming and supportive environment for students extends to all areas of the college. A major focus of our Strategic Plan is ensuring that all students can earn an associate's degree or certificate, seamlessly transfer to a baccalaureate program, or complete a continuum of educational experiences to achieve 21st-century skills. A second major focus is that the college will be a valuable asset to Philadelphia to create a well-educated workforce and globally-competent community. Obviously, our theme is broad and may encompass a variety of projects, including projects that benefit students indirectly and those that involve connecting the college with the larger community in some way.

Forging Teams: Because the ability to work collaboratively as part of a team is such an essential leadership skill, each participant is assigned to a project team. Project teams include members who represent different areas within the college and bring to the table different skills, strengths, perspectives, and capabilities. The teams are a great opportunity to forge working relationships among colleagues who would not ordinarily get the chance to work together.

Forming Alliances: To effectively plan and implement your project, you will be required to work closely with colleagues outside of the Leadership Institute. It is extremely important that you identify and consult with all others who may be directly impacted by your project as well as those who have authority and/or expertise in the area you are pursuing. Developing a network of supportive allies is an essential ingredient for success.

Project Scope: It is important to limit the scope of the project so that planning and implementation can be completed during the coming academic year. For example, if the problem or challenge your project addresses is large in scope, we suggest that you limit your project to one aspect of the problem or use the project to take the initial step in what may turn out to be a long-term effort.

Doing the Research: Basic research into the issue(s) addressed by your project is a requirement. This research should include interviews with college colleagues who have expertise and authority in the area your project addresses. It may also include contacting area institutions to learn how others are tackling your issue. It should include making use of institutional research already conducted by the college, or it may require conducting institutional research of your own.

Library and internet research into the literature on your topic will also form part of the essential foundation for your project proposal. Help with library and internet research strategies can be made available to an individual or team if needed.

Identifying Resources: Although there is no funding available to support projects within the scope of the Leadership Institute, project teams in past years have proven adept at identifying resources already available at the college. These resources have included knowledgeable and supportive colleagues as well as material and financial resources. We would also like to encourage teams to apply for funding through the College Mini-Grant Program during the spring 2014 semester, if appropriate. One of our Leadership Institute fall sessions will feature a panel discussion on grant writing.

The Timeline: The fall semester will be devoted to laying the groundwork for the project by assembling project teams, selecting project ideas, assigning mentors, conducting research of various kinds, identifying internal and external resources, planning a preliminary budget, and planning for project implementation. On January 9, 2014, teams will present project proposals to members of the college community.

The primary focus during the spring 2014 semester will be carrying out the projects by implementing the proposals. Although progress reports will be included on the Program Schedule, each team will construct its own timeline for implementation. The final project reports will be presented at the final session of the Leadership Institute on Friday, April 25, 2014.

August 29	Project Overview
September 20	Project Teams Assigned; Exploring Potential Topics
October 18	Project Topics Selected; Working Plan Initiated
November 22	Research Summaries Due
December 13	Draft Project Proposals Due With Preliminary Budgets
January 9	Project Proposal Presentations to the College Community
February 7	Project Team Work Session
February 28	Project Team Work Session
March 28	Project Progress Reports
April 25	Final Project Reports

Community College of Philadelphia Leadership Institute

Appendix M

Project Overview Guide

I. Role of the group project

- Explore your personal leadership style and how to work within a group.
- Learn to navigate the paths of power at the college.
- Take a fresh approach to existing challenges at the college; seek innovative solutions.
- Look beyond your own corner of the college to consider the broader institutional structure.

II. Managing your time

- Groups are responsible to meet independently to set goals and meet deadlines.
- Schedule time for your project.

  - Consider meeting at the same time/same place to keep pace.
  - Make full use of technology to stay in touch—email, Yahoo/Google groups, calendar software.
  - Define clear roles within the group—spokesperson, researcher, etc.
  - Use whiteboarding for ideas and timeline.

III. Points to consider

- Implementation

- Can your project be done within the time parameters of the Institute?
- How will your project be institutionalized within the college?
- How will the success of your project be assessed?

- Choosing a topic

  - Keep in mind our theme of "Fostering Student Success and Making an Impact."
  - Keep an eye on serving the college community.
  - Look beyond your particular area.
  - Play to your strengths.

IV. Next steps

- You will be assigned to a group.
- Schedule a meeting as soon as your group is assigned.
- Discuss roles.
- Brainstorm ideas.

Suggested Exercise:
Turn to the person next to you and brainstorm possible projects around the college that are not being addressed. Refer to the "Choosing a Topic" section above as a guide. Don't sweat the details too much; just get the wheels going.

Community College of Philadelphia Leadership Institute

Appendix N

Sample Invitation to Project Presentations

Dear Colleagues,

On Thursday, January 9th, from 2:00 to 3:30 p.m. in Rm. S2-3, the Leadership Institute project teams will be presenting their project proposals to members of the college community for questions and feedback. We would like to invite you to attend this session. We believe it is important that the Leadership Institute participants (some of whom are in your areas) have the advantage of presenting their ideas before an audience with expertise and experience in a variety of areas relevant to the various proposals.

This year's proposal topics focus on the theme of fostering student success and making an impact. In brief, the projects are

- ***Sound Off***

    To provide students with a new avenue of communication by which they may give suggestions and express concerns
    Team Members: Names provided

- ***Culture of Advocacy***

    To identify why students most at risk of dropping out may not be utilizing the services in place to help them succeed and, if services are being utilized, how the students experience them
    Team Members: Names provided

- ***CCP 101***

    To provide information, resources, support, and continuous training to Student Affairs staff in order to better assist students in making the transition to college as seamless as possible
    Team Members: Names provided

- ***Steps on the Path—Student Assistance Program***

    To initiate an "addictions meeting" at the college and provide resources for students regarding emotional well-being
    Team Members: Names provided

Ideally, the questions and feedback, provided in a supportive atmosphere by audience members representing the college community, will enable Leadership Institute participants to improve their proposals. In previous years, the feedback from invited guests has proved invaluable in helping participants to more carefully define the scope of the projects, delineate steps to completion, clarify logistics and institutional context, and identify resources of which they may not be aware.

We hope you can attend to provide your input and support to our fellow colleagues on January 9th. Thank you and Happy New Year!

Community College of Philadelphia Leadership Institute

Appendix O

Sample Project Presentation Feedback Form

Please take a few moments to provide feedback to the four project teams using the space provided below. Thank you.

1. Sound Off

This project's primary goal is to provide students with a new avenue of communication by which they may give suggestions and express concerns. The hope is that the opportunity will help relieve some of the everyday frustration that students often experience just because they are dealing with a large institution. We also hope to direct the feedback to appropriate departments to raise consciousness about student issues and perhaps stimulate changes when possible with the goal of improving student retention.
Team Members: Names and departments provided
Mentor: Name provided, Assistant Dean of Students/Director of Student Life

2. Culture of Advocacy

This project aims to identify why students most at risk of dropping out may not be utilizing the services in place to help them succeed and, if services are being utilized, how the students experience them. We will identify areas for improvement within service areas and college-wide. Student/staff interaction is an area that the initiative will evaluate as well. It is hoped that empowering

and equipping staff with the language, resources, and tools for improved student interaction will foster a "culture of advocacy" where students feel their progress is important to those they look to for guidance, assistance, and support.
Team Members: Names and departments provided
Mentor: Name provided, Dean of Students

3. CCP 101

"CCP 101" is a project designed to provide information, resources, support, and continuous training to Student Affairs staff to better assist students, continuing but especially new, in making the transition to college as seamless as possible. Mini courses throughout the academic year will provide information to foster a better understanding of the processes that students must go through to get on the right path. CCP 101 will demonstrate how interdependent the various departments are upon one another.
Team Members: Names and departments provided
Mentor: Name provided, Vice President for Student Affairs

4. Steps on the Path—Student Assistance Program

Two important factors in addressing and recovering from mental health issues are being able to build a network of peers and having access to support services. This project proposes to initiate an addictions meeting at the college. We will assess what is needed to start one, acquire dedicated space, and connect with students who are open in recovery to facilitate. The project will also provide resources for students regarding emotional well-being. Pertinent information will be accessible manually and electronically in a comprehensive resource guide.
Team Members: Names and departments provided
Mentor: Name provided, Faculty, Behavioral Health and Human Services

Name (Optional) _____

Community College of Philadelphia Leadership Institute

Appendix P

Final Report Specs

Each project team will present an oral final report at the last session of the Leadership Institute to LI class members, mentors, and other invited guests. Each team will submit a written report as an MS-Word document, which includes the components listed below. The report should be sent to the co-coordinators and is due prior to the oral reports.

1. Project title and team member names/mentor names
2. An overview of the project proposal/goals
3. An explanation of how the project relates to this year's theme of "Fostering Student Success and Making an Impact"
4. A summary of research undertaken in the completion of the project
5. An outline of steps taken to complete the project
6. For short-term projects, if now completed, an overview of how they turned out
7. For long-term projects, an outline of next steps and long-term goals
8. An overview of how the project has been or may be institutionalized within the college for continuity
9. Assessment results or plans for assessment
10. A summary (from each team member) of what you learned by doing the project and how it impacted you as a leader

Community College of Philadelphia Leadership Institute

Appendix Q

*Sample of Projects Completed at
Community College of Philadelphia*

Suggested Guidelines for the College's Classified/Confidential Staff Professional Development Program

Through the Contract, the college has made a commitment to a more comprehensive staff development program for employee job enrichment that will lead to additional support for students, faculty, administrators, and the entire college community.

"CCP 101"

Assist new students in understanding and navigating the college enrollment process.

"TUBE NEWS"

Develop a continuous loop tape showing the variety of activities, programs, and students on Main campus.

Alumni Speaker Series

Bring together current employers, alumni, faculty, and students. Provide career planning and employment development strategies.

A Guide to Enrolling at CCP

Create a flow chart of the step-by-step process to enrollment.

Improving Communications: Enhancing Quality Customer Service Through Professional Development Training

Help employees better understand what quality customer service is, increase morale, and demonstrate positive customer-service behaviors in daily performance.

The Majors Fair

Empower undecided students to make better choices by increasing their awareness of options regarding majors, programs, degrees, and transfer opportunities.

Men of Color: Path to Power

Increase retention of incoming African American and Hispanic males through a series of seminars on academic and social issues of interest to the group.

The Student Portal Tutorial Project

Develop a tutorial for students on how to use the student portal and how to utilize the resources available to them.

Focus on Core Values: An Awareness and Implementation Campaign of the Student Code of Conduct (Know the Code)

Raise campus awareness of issues related to academic integrity in general and the CCP Student Code of Conduct in particular.

Civility: Focus on Sexual Orientation and Gender Equity

College-wide discussion of sexual orientation and gender equity to help raise consciousness, tolerance, and build civility in our Community College of Philadelphia community.

Utilizing Syllabus Design to Promote Student-Centered Learning

Provide interested faculty with tips and tools to develop a student-centered syllabus. The delivery method will be a presentation to the college community and a web page with syllabi models in addition to links for further information.

CCP VetConnect: An Online Community for Veterans at Community College of Philadelphia

Establish a lounge-like virtual place for veterans to receive relevant information about navigating the college and to communicate with each other on topics of an academic and support nature.

Library Services Video Project

Develop a student-centered video to help students navigate the library and all its resources. This project will serve as a model for other student videos focused on additional resource areas at the college.

Academic Check-Up (Student Affairs Initiative)

Provide self-awareness, increase knowledge of current curricula, and increase retention. All degree-seeking students would be required to schedule an "Academic Check-Up" meeting before earning 24 credit hours to review and revise their educational plan as necessary.

College Etiquette 101

Create video using scenarios to illustrate college etiquette not only in the classroom but also in other areas of the college. The video will illustrate how poor etiquette can be detrimental to the college learning experience.

The CCP Alternative Spring Break

Develop and implement a domestic service-learning project to be held during the college's spring break. Students and chaperones travel to a designated site and assist in the construction of a building or other community service as needed. Students explore the designated area and are exposed to new and different cultures and keep journals during the trip to enhance their writing skills and provide an outlet for reflection.

Sound Off

Provide students with a new avenue of communication by which they may give suggestions and express concerns (a sound-off booth). The hope is that the opportunity will help relieve some of the everyday frustration that students often experience just because they are dealing with a large institution.

Direct the feedback to appropriate departments to raise consciousness about student issues and perhaps stimulate changes when possible with the goal of improving student retention.

Steps on the Path

Two important factors in addressing and recovering from mental health issues are being able to build a network of peers and having access to support services. The project will provide resources for students regarding emotional well-being. Pertinent information will be accessible manually and electronically in a comprehensive resource guide.

Community College of Philadelphia Leadership Institute

Appendix R

Sample Mentor Request Letter

Dear Mentor Name,

Would you be willing to mentor one of our Leadership Institute project teams as they plan and implement their project this year? The theme for this year's projects is "**Fostering Student Success and Making an Impact**." A major challenge facing community colleges nationwide is the fact that many of our students leave us before they have achieved their academic and personal goals. Although researchers have identified teaching strategies that correlate highly with increased student persistence and success, the responsibility for creating a welcoming and supportive environment for students extends to all areas of the college.

As a mentor, you would meet with the members of the project team, as the need arises and as your schedule allows, to provide practical advice to aid in the completion of their project and to provide insights and ideas regarding assessing its impact and in sustaining it beyond the Leadership Institute year.

The project that I think you would be a terrific mentor for is described below. I know that team members have already spoken to you about their idea.

"Steps on the Path — Student Assistance Program"

The team has chosen to focus on initiating a meeting at the college for those in recovery. Their intent is to assess what is needed to start a meeting, acquire dedicated space, and connect with students who are open in recovery to facilitate. They also plan to develop a comprehensive resource guide. The team's research summary is attached.

Project Team Members: Names provided

Thanks for your consideration, Mentor Name, and if you are available on Friday, December 13, from 12:15–1:00 p.m., this would be a great time to have an informal discussion over lunch with the members of the team. We meet in the Boardroom, M2-1.

Appreciatively,

Name

Community College of Philadelphia Leadership Institute

Appendix S

Sample Pre/Post Self-Assessment Tool

Name:_____
Position: ___ Staff ___ Faculty ___ Administrator
___ Full-time ___ Part-time
Date: _____

This self-assessment is designed to help you evaluate your current level of competence and knowledge in areas to be addressed by the Leadership Institute. It will be administered again at the end of the program to enable you to chart your development.

The results will also be compiled, anonymously, for the purpose of assessing the effectiveness of the Leadership Institute.

On a **scale of 1–7, with "1" being lowest and "7" being outstanding**, rate your level of knowledge and skill for each of the items below.

Field and Context Within Which We Work

_____ I understand the college's mission, vision, and values.
_____ I have a good understanding of the organizational structure and culture of the college and how to navigate within it.
_____ I am aware of the expertise and insights of local, state, and national leaders relevant to the mission of the community college.
_____ I understand the complexity and interconnectedness of local, state, and national issues that impact the community college.

_____ I am aware of emerging trends on the local, state, and national levels that might impact the community college.

_____ I understand how external issues and trends relate to my job responsibilities and know how to respond appropriately.

The Nature of Leadership

_____ I am aware of the kinds of research data available from the college's Office of Institutional Research and know how to access it.

_____ I understand basic concepts of resource allocation, budgeting, and finance.

_____ I have basic skills as a grant writer.

_____ I have confidence as a public speaker and presenter.

_____ I know how to assess the effectiveness of my work and consistently do so.

_____ I am confident in interpreting data and using it to make improvements.

_____ I am skilled at managing and resolving conflict.

_____ I have confidence in my ability to make strategic decisions.

_____ I am confident in my ability to deal effectively with issues of diversity in higher education.

_____ I am aware of my own strengths and weaknesses as an individual and leader.

Working With Others

_____ I can work productively as part of a team.

_____ I communicate and listen well.

_____ I understand what motivates people to do their best work.

_____ I am aware of the ways my words, actions, and emotions impact others.

_____ I am a confident and collaborative problem solver.

Community College of Philadelphia Leadership Institute

Appendix T

Session Feedback—Decision Making in Higher Education

Appendix T

Your input is important to us and will help us plan future Leadership Institute activities. Please take a moment to answer the questions below and submit this form to a facilitator before leaving.

Section I. **Please answer the questions using the scale below.**

1	2	3	4	5
Strongly Disagree	Disagree	Unsure or No Opinion	Agree	Strongly Agree

_____ The reading material associated with today's session was relevant and useful.
_____ I was given adequate opportunity to ask questions/offer opinions during today's session.
_____ The presenter(s) was/were well-prepared, effective, and engaging.
_____ Overall, I would recommend today's session to future Leadership Institute participants.

Section II. **Please answer the following questions specific to today's session.**

1. What insights did you gain from today's presentation?

2. What alligators have you faced in your professional life and how did you respond?

3. What is one new decision-making strategy that you would consider using in your job? Or what strategy is working well for you?

Section III. Additional Comments (Please use back of form.)

Community College of Philadelphia Leadership Institute

Appendix U

Rating Summary of Session Topics

Please rate each topic using a scale of 1 to 5 with 1 being least helpful and 5 being most helpful.

Identifying Your Leadership Style and Building Effective Teams
Presenter Name   1   2   3   4   5

Leadership and Change at the Local Level
Presenter Name   1   2   3   4   5

Higher Education at the State Level
College Presidents' Panel
Presenter Names   1   2   3   4   5

Six Thinking Hats: Now We Are Green
Presenter Name   1   2   3   4   5

National Trends
Higher Education Accreditation
Presenter Name   1   2   3   4   5

Grant-Writing Panel Discussion
Presenter Names   1   2   3   4   5

Public Speech for the Polished Professional
Presenter Name   1   2   3   4   5

Team Presentation of Project Proposals to College 1   2   3   4   5

Communication and Conflict Resolution
Presenter Name   1   2   3   4   5

Decision-Making Workshop—Watch Out for Alligators
Presenter Name   1   2   3   4   5

Balancing the Budget: A Case Study
Presenter Name   1   2   3   4   5

Diversity: Walking the Talk
Presenter Name   1   2   3   4   5

Please use the back of the form for any comments you would like to make on any of the session topics. You may also indicate any topics you would add for future programs.

Community College of Philadelphia Leadership Institute

Appendix V

Sample Midpoint Evaluation

Appendix V

Please use this Evaluation Form to indicate how well the Leadership Institute sessions so far have fulfilled the overall goals of the Leadership Institute. Completed online evaluations are due by **January 6th**. We will discuss your feedback at our session on January 9th. *Thank you.*

Part I. Use the scale below to reflect your evaluation. Type the number of your response in the box beside each item. Feel free to add a short comment beneath your rating or to add comments at the end of the evaluation form.

1	2	3	4	5
Strongly Agree	Agree	Don't Know	Disagree	Strongly Disagree

☐ 1. I have interacted with and gained insight from leaders in various fields related to the College's mission.
Comments:

☐ 2. I have an increased awareness of the local, state, and national contexts within which the college functions.
Comments:

☐ 3. I have an increased understanding of specific ways in which the larger environment may impact the college in the pursuit of its mission.
Comments:

☐ 4. I have developed an increased self-awareness as a leader and an understanding of my leadership style
Comments:

☐ 5. I have increased my knowledge of grant writing, specific to CCP.
Comments:

☐ 6. I have more confidence about speaking in a public arena.
Comments:

☐ 7. I feel that I am part of a collaborative network of problem solvers.
Comments:

☐ 8. I have had the opportunity to work collaboratively on a project of interest to me and of benefit to the College community.
Comments:

☐ 9. I have gained a deeper understanding of the College mission, vision and values.
Comments:

Part II. Please write a short paragraph in response to each of the following questions.

10. What is the single most important lesson about leadership you have learned in the Leadership Institute so far?

11. What are your greatest strengths as a leader? Have you developed any new strengths or skills as a result of participation in the Leadership Institute so far?

12. In what ways has the Leadership Institute been most helpful to you so far? In what ways could the Leadership Institute provide more benefit to you?

13. How has the Leadership Institute project been beneficial to your personal/leadership development? Please explain.

14. Do you feel you have had adequate time during the Institute to plan, evaluate, and garner feedback on the projects?

15. In what ways would you like more help with the project? Be as specific as possible.

16. Has your team met with your project mentors? If so, do you believe the information and feedback you received will be beneficial in completing your project? Why or why not?

Additional Comments:

Permission granted by American Association of Community Colleges to use in *Up and Running: Starting and Growing a Leadership Program at a Community College*. (Portions of artifact were previously published in Jeandron, C. A. [2006]. *Growing your own leaders: Community colleges step up*. American Association of Community Colleges. Washington, DC: Community College Press.)

Community College of Philadelphia Leadership Institute

Appendix W

Sample Final Evaluation

Please use this evaluation form to indicate how well the Leadership Institute sessions have fulfilled the overall goals of the Leadership Institute. Completed online evaluations are due by **April 28th**.

Your thoughtful feedback will help to make the Leadership Institute a more powerful experience. *Thank you for your contributions.*

Please respond as fully as possible to the following questions.

1. Have you taken on a new position, new responsibilities, or leadership initiatives at the college or in other organizations since participating in the LI? If so, please describe.

2. Which aspect of the LI had the greatest impact on you?

3. What insight(s) did you gain from leaders you met through the LI?

4. Comment on your growth or any insights gained in such areas as communication, conflict resolution, and decision making.

5. How has your understanding of the organizational culture of the college changed, if at all?

6. How have you applied or how do you see yourself applying your knowledge of resource allocation, budgeting, and finance in your work?

7. How, if at all, do you imagine making use of the connections you formed with LI colleagues?

8. What did you learn from your participation in the team project?

9. How, if at all, have you deepened your understanding of CCP's mission, vision, and values?

10. How have you applied what you have learned in the LI in your current position?

11. Do you feel more willing and prepared to take a greater leadership position? Explain.

12. Have your professional goals changed? If so, how?

13. How would you say you have changed, if at all?

14. What would you change for future participants?

15. As an alumnus(a), how do you imagine you might continue working with the Leadership Institute? What might that look like?

Additional Comments:

Position: ___ Staff ___ Faculty ___ Administration
___ Full-time ___ Part-time

Community College of Philadelphia Leadership Institute

Permission granted by American Association of Community Colleges to use in *Up and Running: Starting and Growing a Leadership Program at a Community College*. (Portions of artifact were previously published in Jeandron, C. A. [2006]. *Growing your own leaders: Community colleges step up*. American Association of Community Colleges. Washington, DC: Community College Press.)

Appendix X

Proposal for Executive Leadership Institute

What's Our Vision?

Why is the ELI important? What is its value? What is the desired conclusion?

We propose the creation of an Executive Leadership Institute (ELI) to provide Leadership Institute (LI) alumni the opportunity to:

- (Re)connect with LI colleagues on an ongoing basis
- Resume research activities and classroom-style discussions on leadership issues
- Resume group project work in service to the college

What's the Institutional Value?

Any project must add measurable value to the college from a "balanced scorecard" perspective.

Financial

The ELI and its connected projects will run and be completed at little or no cost to the college. Individual projects will include information (when applicable) relating to money-generating or cost-saving benefits.

Internal Process

The ELI will serve as a template for showing how teams and departments can work together to improve operations and results.

Customer

ELI project work will focus on improving processes that directly benefit employees and students.

Learning and Innovation

The ELI will build on the LI foundations of personal and professional development. Information and lessons learned will be made available to the entire college to provide guidelines for ongoing, systematic improvement.

What Are the Key Performance Indicators (KPIs)?

1. Year One: ELI members representing 20% of the current LI alumni.
2. Year One: At least one major project (institution-wide) and one minor project (division- or department-wide) will be planned, executed, and reviewed for effectiveness based on projects' established KPIs.
3. Year One: Presentation of ELI activities during Professional Development Week.
4. Year Two: Additional 10% of alumni will join ELI.

What Are the Tactics and Operations?

What is the action plan? Who is responsible? What are the deliverables? What is the time frame?

(*Without this information, you do not have a workable solution, only good intentions.*—Peter Drucker)

Much of the detail work will fall into place once the initial ELI group meets and decides on a management team as well as the format and frequency of meetings. Some initial thoughts:

A. Meeting Structure

A biweekly, one-hour work session (held during lunchtime to minimize interruptions to work schedules). Meetings will be designed to include two primary components.

1. Book Club
   In each session, different ELI members will conduct a discussion, providing exposure to public speaking and team-leading exercises. Depending on the number of participants and the interest in various content, more than one book club group may be formed.
2. Executive Projects

Capitalizing on the "team project" experience from the LI, members will resume group project work. In some cases, two or more groups might work together on different facets of the same project led by a project manager (PM) selected by the group. The PM will be responsible for submitting written and oral reports detailing the results of their team's efforts.

B. Personal Development
Individuals will achieve further leadership development through:

1. Project Management experience
2. Additional teamwork experience
3. Improved communication skills
4. Improved critical-thinking, problem-solving, and decision-making skills

C. Entry Qualifications
New members into the ELI will be considered once per year. Membership is ongoing. Participation is voluntary. Interested candidates must:

1. Be an alumnus of the LI
2. Submit an application including resume and reason for joining ELI

How Will We Monitor Progress?

In conjunction with the Key Performance Indicators, the ELI management team will monitor progress from both a quantitative and qualitative standpoint.

Contributed by Peter Baratta, Leadership Institute alumnus and former coordinator of the Leadership Institute at Community College of Philadelphia

References

American Council on Education (2016, January 15). *New report looks at the status of women in higher education*. Retrieved from http://www.acenet.edu/news-room/Pages/New-Report-Looks-at-the-Status-of-Women-in-Higher-Education.aspx.

Becker, C. (2002, January 25). Trial by fire: A tale of gender and leadership. *The Chronicle of Higher Education*. Retrieved from https://www.chronicle.com/article/Trial-by-Fire-a-Tale-of/20168.

Bennis, W. (2009). *On becoming a leader*. New York: Basic Books.

Beshears, J., & Gino, F. (2015, Winter). Leaders as decision architects. *Harvard Business Review OnPoint*, 106–115.

Brett, J., & Goldberg, S. B. (2017, July 10). How to handle a disagreement on your team. *Harvard Business Review*.

Brubaker, D., Noble, C., Fincher, R., Park, S. K., & Press, S. (2014, Summer). Conflict resolution in the workplace: What will the future bring? *Conflict Resolution Quarterly*, 31(4), 357–386.

Bunch, C. (1979, Summer). Not by degrees: Feminist theory and education. *Quest: A Feminist Quarterly*. Washington, DC.

Caetano, G., Palacios, M., & Patrinos, H. A. (2011, November 18). *Measuring aversion to debt: An experiment among student loan candidates*. Retrieved from https://www2.owen.vanderbilt.edu/miguel.palacios/index_files/CPPMeasuringAvesiontodebt.pdf.

Center for Urban Education. *Developing a practice of equity minded indicators*. Retrieved from https://cue.usc.edu/files/2016/02/Developing-a-Practice-of-Equity-Mindedness.pdf.

Cilliers, F., & Greyvenstein, H. (2012). The impact of silo mentality on team identity: An organizational case study. *SA Journal of Industrial Psychology*, 38(2), Art. #993, 1–9.

De Bono, E. (1999). *Six thinking hats* (rev.). New York: Back Bay Books / Little, Brown and Company.

DeRidder, C. G., & Wilcox, M. A. (1999). *How to improve group productivity: Whole-brain teams set new benchmarks*. Hendersonville, NC: The Brain Connection. http://www.stybelpeabody.com/newsite/pdf/howtoimprovegroupproductivity.pdf.

Druskat, V. U., & Wolff, S. B. (2001, March). Building the emotional intelligence of groups. *Harvard Business Review*.

Ebbers, L., Conover, K., & Samuels, A. (2010, Spring). Leading from the middle: Preparing leaders for new roles. *New Directions for Community Colleges*, 149, 59–64.

Felix, E. R., Bensimon, E. M., Hanson, D., Gray, J., & Klingsmith, L. (2015, Winter). Developing agency for equity-minded change. In E. L. Castro (Ed.), *Understanding Equity in Community College Practice* [Special Issue], 172, 25–42.

Ferdman, B. M. (2014). The practice of inclusion in diverse organizations: Toward a systemic and inclusive framework. In B. M. Ferdman & B. R. Deane (Eds.), *Diversity at work: The practice of inclusion* (pp. 3–54). Hoboken, NJ: John Wiley & Sons.

Flaherty, C. (2017, March 16). Rejecting "campus illiberalism." *Inside Higher Ed.* Retrieved from https://www.insidehighered.com/news/2017/03/16/ideological-odd-couple-robert-george-and-cornel-west-issue-joint-statement-against.

Flaherty, C. (2017, May 9). Divinity, diversity and division. *Inside Higher Ed.* Retrieved from https://www.insidehighered.com/news/2017/05/09/duke-divinity-school-professor-objects-diversity-training-request-and-sets-debate.

Gallegos, P. V. (2014). The work of inclusive leadership. In B. M. Ferdman & B. R. Deane (Eds.), *Diversity at work: The practice of inclusion: Fostering authentic relationships, modeling courage and humility* (pp. 177–202). Hoboken, NJ: John Wiley & Sons.

Hackman, J. R. (2004, June). What makes for a great team? *Psychological Science Agenda.* Retrieved from http://www.apa.org/science/about/psa/2004/06/hackman.aspx.

Herrmann Brain Dominance Instrument. www.herrmannsolutions.com.

Ignatius, A. (Ed.). (2015, Winter). The art of decision making. *Harvard Business Review OnPoint.*

Klein, G. (2007, September). Performing a project premortem. *Harvard Business Review.*

Jeandron, C. A. (2006). *Growing your own leaders: Community colleges step up.* American Association of Community Colleges. Washington, DC: Community College Press.

Johnson, S. K. (2017, August). What 11 CEOs have learned about championing diversity. *Harvard Business Review.*

Lambert, L. M. (2015, March/April). A "grow your own" strategy to develop administrative leadership. *Trusteeship Magazine*, 23(2). Association of Governing Boards of Universities and Colleges. Retrieved from https://www.agb.org/trusteeship/2015/marchapril/a-grow-your-own-strategy-to-develop-administrative-leadership.

Lerner, J. S., Li, Y., Valdesolo, P., & Kassam, K. S. (2015). Emotion and decision making. *Annual Review of Psychology*, 66, 799–823.

Lindsey, A., King, E., Membere, A., & Cheung, H. K. (2017, July). Two types of diversity training that really work. *Harvard Business Review.*

Moss-Racusin, C. A., Molenda, A. K., & Cramer, C. R. (2015). Can evidence impact attitudes? Public reactions to evidence of gender bias in STEM fields. *Psychology of Women Quarterly*, 39(2), 194–209.

Oore, D. G., Leiter, M. P., & LeBlanc, D. E. (2015). Individual and organizational factors promoting successful responses to workplace conflict. *Canadian Psychology*, 56(3), 301–310.

Pekel, J., & Wallace, D. (1998). The ten-step method of decision making. Retrieved from http://managementhelp.org/businessethics/10-Step-Method-Short-Version.pdf.

Pentland, A. (2012, April). The new science of building great teams. *Harvard Business Review.*

Prause, D., & Mujtaba, B. G. (2015). Conflict management practices for diverse workplaces. *Journal of Business Studies Quarterly*, 6(3), 13–22.

Reille, A., & Kezar, A. (2010). Balancing the pros and cons of community college "grow-your-own" leadership programs. *Community College Review*, 38(1), 59–81.

Rock, D., & Grant, H. (2016, November 4). Why diverse teams are smarter. *Harvard Business Review.*

Roese, N. J., & Vohs, K. D. (2012). Hindsight bias. *Perspectives on Psychological Science*, 7(5), 411–426.

Rowland, D. (2016, October 14). Why leadership development isn't developing leaders. *Harvard Business Review.* Reprint H0377k.

Rudgers, L. M., & Peterson, J. L. (2017, January 13). Upcoming trends in 2017 that colleges should prepare for. *Inside Higher Ed.* Retrieved from https://www.insidehighered.com/views/2017/01/13/upcoming-trends-2017-colleges-should-prepare-essay.

Seltzer, R. (2016, September 23). Redoing application reading. *Inside Higher Ed.* Retrieved from https://www.insidehighered.com/news/2016/09/23/demographic-changes-prompt-changes-application-reading.

Shapiro, M. (2015, September 8). Help your team agree on how they'll collaborate. *Harvard Business Review*.

Sherbin, L., & Rashid, R. (2017, February). Diversity doesn't stick without inclusion. *Harvard Business Review*.

Smith, A. A. (2016, May 20). Tension at the top. *Inside Higher Ed*. Retrieved from https://www.insidehighered.com/news/2016/05/20/many-community-college-presidencies-are-upheaval.

Smith, P. M. (2002). *Rules and tools for leaders*. New York: Perigee.

Society for College and University Planning (Spring 2017). *Trends for higher education: Evolution of higher education*. www.scup.org/trends.

Stone, F. (2004). Deconstructing silos and supporting collaboration. *Employment Relations Today*, 31, 11–18. doi:10.1002/ert.20001.

Thompson, P. (2017, January). How mindfulness helped a workplace diversity exercise. *Harvard Business Review*.

Tierney, J. (2011, August 17). Do you suffer from decision fatigue? *The New York Times Magazine*. Retrieved from http://www.nytimes.com/2011/08/21/magazine/do-you-suffer-from-decision-fatigue.html.

Toegel, G., & Barsoux, J. (2016, June). How to preempt team conflict. *Harvard Business Review*.

Tyree, L. W., Milliron, M. D., & de los Santos, G. E. (Eds.). (2004). *The leadership dialogues: Community college case studies to consider*. Phoenix, AZ: League for Innovation in the Community College.

Ullman, E. (2017, June/July). Taking the confusion out of college leadership programs. *Community College Journal*, 87(6), 10–11.

Index

AACC. *See* American Association of Community Colleges (AACC)
acceptance letter, 4, 6; sample of, 83
alumni: follow-up with, 71, 78; further leadership opportunities, 73, 77, 78, 79, 147; independent initiatives, 78–79; network, 79; recruitment resource, 4
American Association of Community Colleges (AACC), xi, 72
application: checklist, 111; sample of, 5, 87
application process, 4; selection committee guidelines, 5, 91; selection criteria, 5–6, 92, 96
assessment: longer term, 74; pre/post, 71, 135. *See also* evaluation
assessment, thinking styles, 18; Myers-Briggs Type Indicator, 18, 22, 26, 27; place in program, 23. *See also* Herrmann Brain Dominance Instrument® Assessment (HBDI® Assessment)

budget: checklist, 111; sample of, 15, 16; savings, 18, 19

CCP. *See* Community College of Philadelphia
coaching, 35, 40, 49
cognitive biases, 54; anchoring, 55, 56; confirmation bias, 55, 56; framing, 55, 56; status quo, 55, 56. *See also* decision making
comments from Leadership Institute participants at CCP, 4, 5, 23, 28, 32, 34, 36, 37, 38, 41–42, 58, 64, 73, 74, 75, 79
Community College of Philadelphia (CCP), lessons from, 6, 12, 31, 33, 34, 35, 37, 38, 40, 41, 65, 75
conflict, types occurring in organizations, 45
conflict resolution: approaches to, 49, 50; factors associated with positive outcomes, 45–46; goals for presentation, 45, 51; presenter choice, 46; techniques for, 49. *See also* Gordon, Thomas A.
coordinator: co-coordinator, 15; roles of, 13, 16, 29, 31, 36, 38, 41, 63, 65, 68, 72, 74, 78; sources, xiii, 15, 78
CNN rule, 60

De Bono, Edward, 31–32. *See also* Six Thinking Hats
decision making: alligator characteristics, 57; case studies for practice, 59, 60; cognitive biases, 54–55, 56; emotions, influences of, 53–54; improving decision making, 57; influences on, 53, 56; pre-mortem technique, 58; presenter choice, 54, 55; ten-step method, 58–59; time of day, influences of, 53, 54

155

diversity. *See* diversity and inclusion
diversity and inclusion: definitions of, 61; hot button issues, 62; inclusive environments, factors of, 62; inclusive leadership, examples of, 65; proactive leadership, 63
diversity presentation resources, 65–66; case studies, 67, 68; equity-minded tools, 66; implicit bias test, 66; lessons from CEOs, 66–67
diversity presentation, steps for, 65; developing the session plan, 68; goals for session, 65; presenter choice, 63, 65; timing in program, 65. *See also* García, Ana Maria

emotional intelligence: group emotional intelligence, 30; group norms for awareness and regulation of emotions, 31, 46; test for, 18
equity-minded tools. *See* diversity presentation resources
evaluation of program: final evaluation, focus of, 73; final evaluation form, sample of, 73, 145; mid-point evaluation form, sample of, 72, 143; mid-point evaluation, purpose of, 72–73; place in program, xvi, 71; post program evaluation, 71; session feedback form, sample of, 72, 138; session feedback, purpose of, 72; summary of sessions, 72, 139

facilities, 19
Familiarity, Comfort and Trust (FCT) approach, 26, 27, 28

García, Ana Maria: model for diversity and change, 63–64; participant responses, 64
Gordon, Thomas A.: approach to presentation on conflict, 46, 49; conflict as catalyst, 47; distortions and confusions about conflict, 48; diversity, honoring and reinforcing, 47; interview with, 46
grow your own (GYO) programs, 33, 40
guidelines: group operational, 9; discussion board, 11–12; selection committee, 5, 91

Hackman, Richard, *Five Factor Model*, 34–35
HBDI® Assessment. *See* Herrmann Brain Dominance Instrument® Assessment (HBDI® Assessment)
Herrmann Brain Dominance Instrument® Assessment (HBDI® Assessment), 22; graphic of average profile, 23, 25; participant comment, 23; Team Planning Walk-Around, 24, 27; Team Ready-for-Action Assessment tool, 24; thinking preferences, 22, 24; Whole Brain® Model, 22, 23, 27, 28, 36
hospitality, 18

inclusion. *See* diversity and inclusion

materials, for program, 16, 18; checklist, 112
mentoring. *See* team projects
Metaphor Exercise, 9, 10

Name Tent Exercise, 9

presenters, 10–11, 13, 16, 17, 18, 103
president of college, role of, 4, 7, 11, 112
program planning, checklist for, 13, 111
public speaking, 12

readings, 8, 11, 107; discussion guidelines, 12
recruitment, 3, 19
rejection letter, 4; sample of, 85

schedule: checklist, 111; program sessions, 8, 10, 11, 19, 88, 89; sample of, 97; sessions, sequence of, 12
shadowing experience, 12, 13
Six Thinking Hats, 31–32, 114, 115; participant comments, 32
speakers. *See* presenters
Stellato, Deb Cummins: 80/20 rule, 29; facilitation role, 30; insights gained, 29; interview with, 24; silo effect, 28; take-aways about thinking style, 28; toxic people, 29. *See also* Familiarity, Comfort and Trust (FCT) approach

sustainability of program, xvi, 4, 71

team building: effectiveness of teams, 22, 30, 31; relationship to thinking styles, 21. *See also* assessment, thinking styles; Hackman, Richard, *Five Factor Model*; Stellato, Deb Cummins, interview with

team projects: benefits of, 33, 75; diversity of teams, 33, 35; feedback, 40, 125; final reports, 40; mentoring, 35, 40, 133; presentation of proposals, 39; project directive, 37, 117; project funding, 38; project overview guide, 37, 121; sample of projects, 129; scope of, 38; steps to developing, 34; structure and support, 37, 38, 39

thinking styles. *See* assessment, thinking styles

About the Authors

Dr. **Susan J. Tobia** most recently served as assistant vice president for Academic Affairs at Community College of Philadelphia (CCP). Responsibilities included development and coordination of professional development for the college and for new faculty, oversight of the office of academic assessment and evaluation, supervision of the college's three regional centers, and oversight of transfer programs. She served as chair or member of numerous committees at the college, most recently as co-chair of the Middle States Self-Study. In 2003, Dr. Tobia completed an American Council on Education Fellowship whose purpose is to develop leaders in higher education. She was a co-developer of the Leadership Institute at CCP and for 11 years served as lead coordinator. The Leadership Institute was a finalist for the 2005 Bellwether Award and was featured in a book about community college leadership programs. Dr. Tobia was a participant in the American Association of Community Colleges Leading Forward Initiative—*Grow Your Own Programs*, funded by the W. K. Kellogg Foundation. Dr. Tobia earned a BA from Newton College (Massachusetts) in psychology, an MEd from Temple University in Philadelphia in special education, and a PhD in the psychology of reading, also from Temple.

Dr. **Judith L. Gay** currently serves as vice president for Strategic Initiatives and Chief of Staff at Community College of Philadelphia. Prior to assuming her present position, she served the college for 15 years as vice president for Academic Affairs and served as interim president of the college for 10 months during the presidential search process. She was department chair and full professor of psychology at Chestnut Hill College in Philadelphia before assuming community college administrative leadership positions. Under her leadership, Community College of Philadelphia started new initiatives such as the Leadership Institute, created the first academic master plans, and expanded online learning, among other accomplishments. Dr. Gay has held leadership positions beyond the college including with the Middle States Commission on Higher Education and the Delaware Valley Association of Black Psychologists. She also served as a member of the American Council on Education's Leadership Commission. Currently she serves as chair of the board for Interim House, chair of the Higher Education Committee for the Philadelphia Academies, Inc., co-chair of the City of Philadelphia's Running Start Committee, board member for the Philadelphia Education Fund, and Academic Advisory Committee Member for Chestnut Hill College. Dr. Gay holds a BA in psychology from Findlay College (Ohio) and an MA and PhD in experimental psychology from Bowling Green State University in Ohio.

www.ingramcontent.com/pod-product-compliance
Lightning Source LLC
Chambersburg PA
CBHW020740230426
43665CB00009B/499